Making Homes

Home
Series Editors: Victor Buchli and Rosie Cox

ISSN: 2398-3191

This exciting new series responds to the growing interest in the home as an area of research and teaching. Highly interdisciplinary, titles feature contributions from across the social sciences, including anthropology, material culture studies, architecture and design, sociology, gender studies, migration studies and environmental studies. Relevant to undergraduate and postgraduate students as well as researchers, the series will consolidate the home as a field of study.

Food, Masculinities, and Home: Interdisciplinary Perspectives
edited by Michelle Szabo and Shelley Koch

Sexuality and Gender at Home: Experience, Politics, Transgression
edited by Brent Pilkey, Rachael M. Scicluna, Ben Campkin
and Barbara Penner

FURTHER TITLES FORTHCOMING

Making Homes

Ethnography and Design

**SARAH PINK,
KERSTIN LEDER MACKLEY,
ROXANA MOROŞANU,
VAL MITCHELL AND
TRACY BHAMRA**

Bloomsbury Academic
An imprint of Bloomsbury Publishing Plc

B L O O M S B U R Y
LONDON · OXFORD · NEW YORK · NEW DELHI · SYDNEY

Bloomsbury Academic

An imprint of Bloomsbury Publishing Plc

50 Bedford Square
London
WC1B 3DP
UK

1385 Broadway
New York
NY 10018
USA

www.bloomsbury.com

BLOOMSBURY and the Diana logo are trademarks of
Bloomsbury Publishing Plc .

First published 2017

British Library Cataloguing-in-Publication Data
A catalogue record for this book is available from the British Library.

ISBN: HB: 978-1-4742-3915-8
PB: 978-1-4742-3914-1
ePDF: 978-1-4742-3919-6
ePub: 978-1-4742-3917-2

Library of Congress Cataloging-in-Publication Data
A catalog record for this book is available from the Library of Congress.

Cover design: Clare Turner
Cover image © Shotshop GmbH / Alamy Stock Photo

Series: Home

To find out more about our authors and books visit www.bloomsbury.com.
Here you will find extracts, author interviews, details of forthcoming events
and the option to sign up for our newsletters.

Typeset by Deanta Global Publishing Services, Chennai, India
Printed and bound in Great Britain

Contents

List of figures

List of authors

Sarah Pink is Distinguished Professor and Director of the Digital Ethnography Research Centre at RMIT University, Australia. She is Visiting Professor across the Schools of Design and Civil and Building Engineering at Loughborough University, UK, and International Visiting Professor at Halmstad University, Sweden. Her research brings together theoretical and academic scholarship with applied practice through design ethnography approaches to understanding and creating interventions in everyday life. Her most recent books include: *Anthropologies and Futures* (2017), *Theoretical Scholarship and Applied Practice* (2017), *Digital Ethnography: Principles and Practice* (2016), *Digital Materialities* (2016), *Screen Ecologies* (2016), *Doing Sensory Ethnography*, 2nd edition (2015), and *Media, Anthropology and Public Scholarship* (2015). Her research has been funded by National Research Councils in the United Kingdom, Spain, Australia and Sweden and through the EU Horizon 2020 programme, as well as through partnerships with companies including Unilever (United Kingdom), Intel (the United States), Volvo Cars (Sweden), Suncorp (Australia), and other organizations.

Kerstin Leder Mackley is a Senior Research Associate at UCL's London Knowledge Lab, working on the IN-TOUCH: Digital Touch Communication project. She has previously held research posts at the Loughborough Design School, the Department of Social Sciences, Loughborough University, and the School of Engineering and Design, Brunel University. Kerstin's background is in audience and reception research from a broad media and cultural studies perspective. She has applied a keen interest in people, emerging technologies and everyday life to a range of sustainability projects, including energy demand reduction (LEEDR – Low Effort Energy Demand Reduction, 2010–14) and hot water consumption (Hothouse, 2014–17). Her ethnographic work has informed interdisciplinary research challenges and built on the intersections between anthropology, engineering, user-centred design and applied futures research. Kerstin has published in a variety of peer-reviewed journals, including *Media, Culture & Society*, *TOCHI* and the *Journal of Design Research*.

Roxana Moroşanu is a research associate at the University of Cambridge, UK. She completed a PhD in social anthropology at Loughborough University in 2014. Roxana works at the intersection between the fields of social sciences of sustainability, digital anthropology, design anthropology and the new sociology of art. Her current research looks at creativity and fixation in designers' work. She has published in a variety of peer-reviewed journals, including *The Cambridge Journal of Anthropology*, *International Journal of Cultural Studies*, and *TOCHI*. Her most recent book is *An Ethnography of Household Energy Demand in the UK: Everyday Temporalities of Digital Media Usage* (2016). Together with Felix Ringel, she edited the special issue 'Time-tricking: Reconsidering Temporal Agency in Troubled Times' for *The Cambridge Journal of Anthropology* (March 2016).

Val Mitchell is a senior lecturer in user-experience design at Loughborough Design School, Loughborough University, UK. Her PhD entitled 'Methods for Exploring User Needs for Future Mobile Products and Services' was conducted in collaboration with a major UK manufacturer of mobile communication technologies. Her research focusses on developing methods and tools for user-centred design and user-experience design, particularly in relation to interdisciplinary research and practice. Her research has been funded by the UK government and research councils as well as commercial organizations. She has published in a variety of peer-reviewed HCI and design journals, including *ACM Transactions on Computer-Human Interaction* (*TOCHI*), *Interacting with Computers*, *Personal and Ubiquitous Computing*, *Co-design* and *The Design Journal*.

Tracy Bhamra is Professor of Sustainable Design and Pro Vice-Chancellor (Enterprise) at Loughborough University, UK. She has a BSc and MSc in manufacturing systems engineering and completed a PhD in design for disassembly and recycling at Manchester Metropolitan University in 1995. In 2003 she established the Sustainable Design Research Group at Loughborough University that undertakes world-leading research in areas such as design for sustainable behaviour, methods and tools for sustainable design, sustainable product service system design and sustainable design education. Her research has been funded by the UK government and research councils and by a number of large industrial organizations. Her book *Design for Sustainability: A Practical Approach* was published in 2007. Tracy is a chartered engineer (CEng) and a Fellow of the Institution of Engineering & Technology (FIET), the Design Research Society (DRS) and the Royal Society for the Encouragement of Arts, Manufactures & Commerce (FRSA).

Acknowledgements

The research discussed in this book was based on in-depth ethnographic and design projects. We would like to thank all of the people who have participated in these studies and made our work possible. Original research discussed in this book was based on the interdisciplinary 'Low Effort Energy Demand Reduction' (LEEDR) project. LEEDR was based at Loughborough University and was jointly funded by the UK Research Councils' Digital Economy and Energy programmes (grant number EP/I000267/1). Where relevant we have drawn on our own unpublished research within this project to present research findings. We have also discussed already published findings from this project and, where relevant, guided readers to the full publications and acknowledged other researchers involved in this project, including Carolina Escobar-Tello, Garrath Wilson and Richard Buswell (PI), whom we would like to particularly acknowledge. In other cases we have discussed existing work on which we have collaborated with others, which has already been published and is therefore available. We have acknowledged the work of colleagues through our references to these joint publications in this book. Here we note these projects to acknowledge the range of collaborative research activity that forms the background to the ideas discussed in this book. These mainly refer to the following projects: the Complex, Clever, Cool (2014–15) project, on which the *Laundry Lives* documentary was based, was developed by Sarah Pink with colleagues in the Digital Ethnography Research Centre at RMIT University, in partnership with Unilever. *Laundry Lives* (2015) was co-directed by Sarah Pink and Nadia Astari; the 'Cleaning Homes & Lifestyles' and 'UK Tablets' study were developed during Sarah Pink's earlier collaborations with Unilever; Sarah Pink was a CI on the 'Management of OSH in Networked Systems of Production or Service Delivery: Comparisons between Healthcare, Construction and Logistics' project, which was funded by IOSH, UK, with PI Alistair Gibb and in this book we refer to publications developed by Sarah Pink with Jennie Morgan and CI Andrew Dainty who developed the ethnographic strand of the wider project; the 'Locating the Mobile' project was funded by an Australian Research Council Linkage Grant with Intel (LP130100848), (2013–16) with chief investigators Larissa Hjorth, Heather Horst and Sarah Pink and international partner investigators Genevieve Bell, Baohua Zhao and

Fumitoshi Kato; 'Sensing, Shaping, Sharing' (2014-17) is funded by the Swedish Research Council with CI's Vaike Fors, Martin Berg and Tom O'Dell; the project 'Consumer-Appealing Low Energy Technologies for Building Retrofitting' (CALEBRE) (EP/G000387/1) was funded by EPSRC & E.ON, with PI Dennis Loveday and RA Val Mitchell; and the 'Carbon, Control and Comfort: User-centred Control Systems for comfort, carbon saving and energy management' (CCC) (EP/G000395/1) was funded by EPSRC & E.ON with PI David Shipworth UCL and CI Tracy Bhamra.

Series preface: Why home?

Rosie Cox and Victor Buchli

The home is where people are made and undone. As life is increasingly seen as precarious, fluid, mobile and globalised, there is a growing interest in the home: what it is, what it means to various groups of people, how it constitutes them, and how it relates to other spheres of life both in the present and in the past. Home is both physical and metaphorical, local and national, a place of belonging and of exclusion. It is at the heart of the most seemingly mundane spaces and experiences - the site of quotidian activities such as eating, washing, raising children, and loving. Yet it is precisely the purportedly banal nature of the home that masks its deep importance for the underlying assumptions that structure social and political life. Home reveals the importance of routine activities, such as consumption to highly significant and urgent wide ranging issues and processes such as the maintenance of and challenges to global capitalism and our relationship to the natural environment.

Amongst academic writers home is increasingly problematised, interrogated and reconsidered. Long understood as an axis of gender inequality, home is also seen as a site for the making of class, racial and ethnic identities; a space of negotiation and resistance as well as oppression and a place where such relationships are undone as well as made. As a topic of study it is the natural analytical unit for a number of disciplines and with relevance to a wide range of cultural and historical settings. The home is probably one of the few truly universal categories upon which an interdisciplinary programme of research can be conducted and which over recent years has resulted in a distinctive analytical category with relevance across disciplines, times and cultures.

This book series offers a space to foster these debates and to move forward our thinking about the home. The books in this series range across the social and historical sciences, drawing out the cross-cutting themes and interrelationships within writings on home and providing us with new perspectives on this intimate space. While our understanding of 'home' is expansive, and open to interrogation, it is not unbounded. In honing our understandings of what 'home' is, this series aims to disturb and it goes beyond the domestic including to sites and states of dispossession and homelessness and experiences of the 'unhomely'.

1

Design, ethnography and homes

Making Homes is a book for researchers and designers who wish to engage with the home as a site for change. The home is an everyday context where interventions that seek to address key issues of societal importance ranging from climate change and environmental sustainability to gender equality, safety, environmental health, social work (and others) are frequently focused. For scholars from many academic disciplines – including anthropology, human geography, cultural studies, design and sociology – the home is a key research site. Home is where we experience significant moments of our lives and celebrate the rituals that punctuate the cycles and rhythms of our social worlds. It is also, importantly, where the intimate and mundane aspects of our lives are lived out. It is the site of those activities that people do not tell others about, perhaps because they are private, because they do not think that they are worth mentioning or because they feel too painful to recount. Yet it is precisely how we habitually live out our lives with the material, sensory, atmospheric and digital configurations of our homes that contributes to the key societal issues that social scientists and designers alike seek to confront.

Domestic life and its everyday mundane activities – such as using digital technologies, doing the laundry, showering and bathing, cooking and cleaning, listening to music or working from home – form the site where habitual but infrequently discussed aspects of everyday life play out. These activities create direct demand for key resources such as electricity, gas and other energy sources and water. Everyday life activity also depends on infrastructures to support it, and appropriate technologies, skills and ways of knowing for its enactment. In these everyday life activities moreover relationships of gender and power are lived out and contested, and food and health pleasures, choices and needs are experienced. Research and design that seeks to make change in or through homes connects not simply with what happens

(a)

(b)

FIGURE 1.1 *Laundry, like showering and working and creating from home, is among the mundane, little spoken about but habitual elements of everyday life in the home. These activities also create part of the materiality and sensoriality of the home and are part of the routines and accomplishments that enable us to create a sense of everyday well-being. Figure 1.1a is a still image from the film* Laundry Lives *(Pink and Astari Dir. 2015) © Sarah Pink and Nadia Astari. Figure 1.1b © LEEDR.*

(a)

(b)

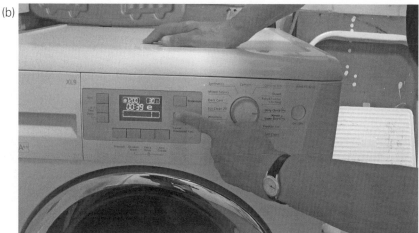

FIGURE 1.2 *Different water and energy infrastructures are implicated in different (and changing) configurations of everyday contingencies and therefore invite possibilities for design and intervention that are equally contingent and contextual. For example, design interventions in Indonesia (above) would need to account for contexts different from those in the UK (below). Ethnographic research reveals ways of knowing about and understanding such differences. Figure 1.2a is a still from the film* Laundry Lives *(Pink and Astari Dir. 2015) © Sarah Pink and Nadia Astari. Figure 1.2b © LEEDR.*

inside homes but with the local, national and global networks of production, consumption and demand, and the infrastructures that they are enmeshed in. The appliances, services, resources and products we (think we) need to have in our homes are part of a global economy of production, distribution and consumption that likewise consumes resources in the making, transportation and distribution of these goods. *Making Homes* puts the home and the people whose everyday activities contribute to its constitution at the centre of this story. Taking the home as site for research, design and intervention, we do not see it as the only place where changes need to be made. Rather we regard it as one entry point into the future-making processes that might lead us to a more sustainable, equitable and healthier world and lives. To achieve this, through both design and ethnography, the focus is on working in collaboration with people, as inhabitants and makers of their homes, to bring about change.

The central issue addressed in this book, therefore, revolves around the question: How can we best go about researching, understanding and designing for change in and through the home? We argue that to engage with the home as a site for future-making, change and intervention, researchers and practitioners need to attend to the home as a changing digital and sensory environment and to work with the creative and improvisatory capacities of people as they live out their everyday lives. These vary across different cultural and national contexts, are themselves ongoingly changing and shape the dynamics of any future-making project.

Making Homes, therefore, argues for a methodology for understanding the home and people that unites the past-present tense of in-depth ethnographic

FIGURE 1.3 *The Energy and Digital Living website discusses a sensory ethnography methodology of design ethnography research in homes, design practice and digital prototypes for interventions in everyday life in the home and hosts a video archive.* © *LEEDR.*

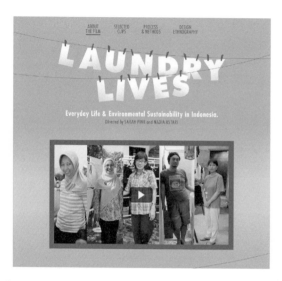

FIGURE 1.4 *The* Laundry Lives *website at www.laundrylives.com includes a trailer and clips from the film, as well as discussions relating to its status as a design ethnography film.* © Sarah Pink and Nadia Astari 2015.

research with the future orientation of design to rework how we understand the temporalities, environments and human activities of the home. It presents new knowledge about how everyday life in the home is lived out. For instance, we discuss examples of the usually hidden processes through which people go to bed at night or do their laundry. The book also presents proposals for how we might, with participants, catalyse change in such contexts through design interventions. For this, we suggest a coherent theoretical and methodological framework, which addresses and advances the needs of a current research environment by understanding the home as a site for *research* and *intervention*. A number of examples we discuss are based on our collective four-year project, the UK-based 'Low Effort Energy Demand Reduction' (LEEDR). We were part of the LEEDR ethnography (Sarah Pink, Kerstin Leder Mackley and Roxana Moroşanu) and design (Val Mitchell and Tracy Bhamra) teams within an interdisciplinary project of up to seventeen people at times. Many examples discussed here are supported by video clips that have been archived in our Energy and Digital Living website, at http://energyanddigitalliving.com/, and we encourage readers to explore the site alongside reading this book.

The examples are often discussed further in peer-refereed journal articles, online videos or documentary. We cite these throughout the book and invite readers to turn to them for more specialized discussions of the subject matter and theoretical and methodological development. Journal articles play an important role in research that bridges scholarly and applied fields. They are where we can debate our project findings to produce novel insights that advance scholarship and design. This book differs from our existing academic

FIGURE 1.5 *The documentary video* Laundry Lives *(2015) is a design ethnography film, directed by Sarah Pink and Nadia Astari, and filmed in Indonesia. The film follows five participants and their households as they explore the challenges and contingencies of their everyday encounters with laundry, washing machines and water. Video still from the film* Laundry Lives *(Pink and Astari Dir. 2015). © Sarah Pink and Nadia Astari 2015.*

publications because it brings together and draws on existing published articles, books and audiovisual work from a range of projects that we have undertaken ourselves, in collaboration with others, or that others have published. These include our work on LEEDR, the documentary film *Laundry Lives* (Pink and Astari 2015) made in Indonesian homes and its website at www.laundrylives. com, Pink's work with Indonesians in their homes in Australia (Pink and Postill 2016) and earlier work, such as Pink's *Home Truths* (2004) about everyday life and gender in UK and Spanish homes. We also draw on projects, including Pink's collaborative research into workers' experiences of other people's homes in the United Kingdom (e.g. Pink, Morgan and Dainty 2015), and into uses of mobile media in intergenerational households in Australia (Pink, Sinanan, Hjorth and Horst, Pink, Hjorth, Horst and Sinanan 2017), as well as Bhamra and Mitchell's research in other energy and home projects (e.g. Mallaband, Haines and Mitchell 2013; Lilley, Bhamra, Haines and Mitchell 2010). Other examples outlined and discussed are drawn from the published work of other researchers working across sociology, human geography, anthropology and design. In this book we present these works in an accessible form for interdisciplinary researchers. Our writing here is always based on thorough critical theoretical and empirical research; however, we have sought to present our findings and arguments to both communicate across anthropology and design, and to be available to other scholars, researchers and students who may not be familiar with the critical fields of enquiry in these disciplines.

In this introduction to *Making Homes* we set the scene. We next map out the most pertinent connections that have already been made between social science and design. We situate the approach advocated here in relation to these. We then examine the concept of home and focus in on it as a site for research, design and change-making and outline a design ethnography approach to the home.

Social science and design

While we acknowledge there is a longer and broader history of relationships between the social sciences and design research and practice, here we focus on approaches that connect social science and design theory, research and practice, developed during the first decades of the twenty-first century. These have emerged through relationships and debates between sociological, anthropological and psychological approaches to understanding the world. They include the subdiscipline of design anthropology (e.g. Gunn and Donovan 2012; Gunn, Otto and Smith 2013); what in Human Computer Interaction (HCI) design has been called the third paradigm (Harrison et al. 2007, 2011) or third-wave HCI (Bødker 2006; Sengers et al. 2009), which is a phenomenologically inspired approach whereby designing is seen as a situated and constructive activity of meaning-making and meaning construction (Ylirisku et al. 2009; Pink et al. 2014); a relationship between science and technology studies (STS) and speculative design (e.g. Michaels 2016); and the use of sociological practice theory in design research (e.g. Shove et al. 2007; Kuijer et al. 2013; Lopes and Gill 2015). Each of these relationships has a set of critical implications for how we interpret design practice and policy. They have also each been applied to research and design in, for or with people in relation to homes, which makes them particularly pertinent to the discussion here.

In recent years design anthropology has become increasingly popular and established. It has been particularly important in informing Sarah Pink's collaborative research in homes, discussed in this book. Alison Clarke has (2010) highlighted a material culture studies approach to design anthropology, which, she proposed, represented a 'seismic shift in the way experts and users conceptualize, envisage, and engage in object culture' (2010: 9). She has suggested that her edited volume revealed that 'contemporary design ... is as much about the spaces, interactions, and meanings between things and people as it is about things themselves' (2010: 9). The digital was also on the agenda for Clarke's vision of design anthropology, which argued, 'Digital anthropology and interaction design are poised to move the theorizing and practice around 21st century object culture' (2010: 13). Here we also engage with digital anthropology (see Horst and Miller 2012) and digital ethnography

(Pink, Horst et al. 2016) to advance the relationship between design and ethnography (Pink, Ardevol and Lanzeni 2016); it would be difficult to undertake design ethnography in homes without attending to how they are experienced and constituted as a digital material environment.

The work of Wendy Gunn and Jared Donovan (2012), Gunn and Ton Otto and Rachel Charlotte Smith (2013) and Sarah Pink (2014) draws on Tim Ingold's ideas to explore design and making (e.g. Ingold 2012, 2013) through a phenomenological approach to design anthropology. These initiatives share resemblances with phenomenological approaches to co-design, developed by Yoko Akama and Alison Prendiville (2013), and the bringing together of design and ethnography as a blended practice, rather than the joining of two separate initiatives (Pink, Akama and Fergusson et al. 2017; Pink, Akama et al. 2015). However as Smith and Mette Gislev Kjærsgaard suggest there is a difference between an anthropological disciplinary approach and one that is ethnographic in that 'design ethnography, as participatory design, focus[ed] on "getting closer" or "drawing things together"', whereas (for them) 'design anthropology [is] ... as much about contextualising these "things," framing and re-framing the objects and practices of design, using different theoretical positionings and critical approaches to explore possible and alternative futures' (Smith and Kjærsgaard 2015). While ethnography can never be practised as absolutely free of theory, the distinction is useful since it enables us to distinguish between approaches where theory is explicitly engaged and developed, where it informs design and ethnographic practice, and where theory is emergent from dialogues with ethnographic and design practice. For instance, in HCI research, ethnomethodological approaches are often used to study the home to create descriptive accounts of everyday life (e.g. Crabtree and Rodden 2004), whereas in sociological social practice theory approaches to design, there are examples of how design is theory led (e.g. Kuijer et al. 2013); and in our own work discussed later in the book, we have used theoretical concepts to inform research design, but have then dialogued with and adapted these through the ethnographic process and used some of these emergent concepts in design practice. In the following chapters we demonstrate how anthropological theory can participate in these discussions, by drawing on anthropological theories of temporality, environment and activity both to understand what happens in homes and to reflect on the ways of knowing that emerge from bringing together design and ethnographic practice.

In contrast to the more scholarly agenda of design anthropology, anthropology, ethnography and design were brought together purposefully in HCI research in relation to the applied needs of the HCI community, rather than to form a subdiscipline. Its earlier manifestations crystallized around Lucy Suchman's work with anthropology and ethnography at the Xerox Palo Alto Research Centre in the 1980s and influenced design anthropology more broadly (e.g. Clarke 2010; Otto and Smith 2013). The initial interests in workplace interactions that characterized this field have broadened to include digital technologies in the home (Bell et al. 2005; Dourish and Bell 2011). The calls of leading researchers, such as Paul Dourish, known for influentially arguing for ethnography to be seen as more than offering 'implications for design' (Dourish 2006, 2007, as cited by Otto and Smith 2013: 7), have been significant. Dourish's emphasis on 'the link between design and critical reflection, and the potential of anthropology in this', and in pointing 'to the transformative potential of classical anthropological studies for understanding relations between people and technologies anew' (Otto and Smith 2013: 8), was an example of a potential role for anthropology. For instance, Irani and Dourish (2009) suggested design may benefit from a colonial studies approach to culture, and Lindtner, Anderson and Dourish (2012) argued for a transnational studies approach in design. Similarly Pink has drawn from migration research, in design ethnography research about technology use in homes (Pink and Postill 2016). Here we call for a design practice that accounts for an anthropology of home and digital technologies and media.

A relationship between theory and ethnography is core to the practice of anthropology and can be explained as an ethnographic-theoretical dialogue (Pink and Morgan 2013), whereby theoretical modes of understanding are adapted and crafted in relation to emerging ethnographic ways of knowing. In the research process we advocate, theory thus informs the research design and interpretation but is always critically reviewed through ethnography to build new theory. For example during our research into digital media, energy demand and everyday life in the home in the United Kingdom, we found that in addition to the usual categories of media research focusing on media as content and as communication, media presence was another important element in the home lives of research participants (Pink and Leder Mackley 2013). This led to the concept of media as presence, and our argument that everyday life is 'saturated' with media beyond the ubiquity of media content, whereby the ubiquity of media being in ambiguous states of on, off or standby modes was also part of the environment of home. The process of bringing together ethnography and design involved using the ethnographic findings to produce new theoretical understandings of the meaning and use of digital media and energy demand in the home, which then enabled us to inform design interventions in novel ways. This principle underpins the relationship between ethnography, design and homes advocated here. However we argue for opening out of such an approach beyond a design *anthropology* approach towards a more interdisciplinary theory-building. This involves engaging critically and generatively with theoretical developments across other disciplines, including human geography and sociology, which we draw on in the following chapters.

Disciplinary theory and design practice are brought together differently in other disciplines, with different potential and limitations. For example, our LEEDR project was undertaken in the domestic energy demand reduction research field, which has generated considerable attention from sociologists and human geographers. Sociologies, psychologies and geographies of energy demand respond with different disciplinary priorities and methods, and critical evaluations of the research 'problem'. These disciplines provide valuable insights into how the problem of climate change, energy demand and consumption is constituted, as well as different theoretical approaches to understanding how it is lived out in homes, and how design interventions should be theoretically informed. No theory is *better* than another in any absolute sense, nevertheless it *matters* which theory one ascribes to because theoretical approaches to understanding the world are attached to certain politics of the everyday, to regimes of governance and regulation, and some theories resonate more clearly with experience of the everyday. Some theories better explain how change has already happened, while others offer convincing ways of comprehending the ongoing processes through which change occurs. Each theory offers one road into the world, because it opens a window onto reality through a particular prism. However, one of the interdisciplinary obstacles here can be that designers and social scientists tend to work differently with theory. For designers theories are useful when they help create a viable intervention in the world. In design, therefore, theory is particularly useful when it helps frame a problem which can be responded to through design or provides a novel reframing of a problem, which helps identify new opportunities for innovation. In contrast, for social scientists theory is a field of ongoing debate, a matter of disciplinary identity and a site for critique of other scholars, of policies, structures and forms of governance.

A comparison of how we understand the home, and design for the home through phenomenological anthropology and sociological uses of social practice theory field (Pink et al. 2013, 2015) shows how different disciplines imply different types of intervention. There are several iterations and applications of notions of 'practice' in the social sciences (see Postill 2010; Pink et al. 2015); however, a particular rendering of practice theory has been advanced through collaborations between sociologists and designers (e.g. Shove et al. 2007), which builds on social practice theory developed by philosophers such as Theodore Schatzki (e.g. Schatzki 2001) and adapted to the sociology of consumption by Alan Warde (2005, 2013). At the risk of oversimplification, here practices are the central building blocks through which the social world, knowledge, skills and practical activity are understood. Practices are seen as 'arrays of activity' (Schatzki 2001: 2) and part of a 'field of practice' in terms of 'the total nexus of interconnected human practices'. This sociological approach often studies practices in the forms of 'entities' and 'performances' (see Warde 2005; Shove et al. 2012). In the context of research about the home, laundry, showering and a range of other activities are regarded as practices. In design research such practices can be used as units to be changed through design interventions. For example, Lenneke Kuijer has explored, through experimental design research projects, the prospect of designing new showering practices (e.g. Kuijer et al. 2013), and other researchers have examined how theories of practice can become embedded in design (e.g. Lopes and Gill 2015). The concept of a practice offers social scientists and designers a ready-made unit of activity to analyse, since it suggests that the object of analysis for researchers, and the entity that designers would seek to change, is a practice or cluster of practices.

There are two core differences between this 'practice theory' approach and the anthropological approach to ethnography and design we advocate here. For instance, although they differ in other ways, the material culture studies and phenomenological anthropology approaches to design anthropology noted above do not predetermine the method of research and analysis as social practice theory does. A material culture studies approach takes a focus on material culture, but it is not interested so much in material objects as its particular unit of analysis, as it is in remaining open to finding out what happens around these objects. Thus, it might not ultimately be the objects themselves that are as significant for design as the social relationships that happen in relation to them. An approach drawn from phenomenological anthropology is also theoretically informed. For example, Wendy Gunn and Christian Clausen have followed a theorization of improvisation developed by Tim Ingold and Elizabeth Hallam (Ingold and Hallam 2007), suggesting that it is through improvisation that people 'find ways of keeping on going' (2013: 174). This enables 'an open-ended approach to innovation where processes of uncertainty and continuous reframing are keys to innovation instead of sources of unwanted uncertainty' (2013: 174). Yet taking such a theory of human action as a starting point does not predetermine that a particular, and consistently replicated, unit of analysis would dominate the design of the research or predetermine what would be designed. Approaches that rely on anthropological ethnography tend to be open to being refigured by what is not yet known. Indeed a core principle of anthropological research practice as developed here involves accepting that the uncertainty of what will be known through ethnography is central to research (Strathern 2000; Amit 2000; Pels 2000; Pink 2016; Pink, Akama et al. 2015). In contrast, if a researcher seeks to study how people perform everyday practices in the home, then she or he is likely to find such practices. Likewise if designers are offered examples of how certain practices are carried out, then they might seek to change these practices in everyday life. Such an approach to research design and approach to intervention depends on the actual existence of practices in real life. Therefore it risks attending insufficiently to the fact that a practice is not necessarily an already existing entity to be found in everyday life, then analysed and redesigned. Instead, the practices that researchers find are drawn together from bits of activity, hunches, interviews – what they are told, and observations – what they see. They become practices because they are brought together to constitute that unit of research and analysis, not necessarily because they exist as a circumscribed set in everyday lived experience. Therefore it is difficult to redesign practices as a method for change-making in the everyday real world. Because this approach is led by a theory of social practices that predetermines what is done as practices, it leaves little scope for a critical re-evaluation of how to best categorize what has been found in the world in order to be able to design in it. As we advocate in this book, a more open process leaves the question of what will be designed more open and enables ethnographic concepts and insights to become part of determining this.

Another approach that brings together social science and design seeks less to find ways to actually bring about change through intervention but attempts more to create speculative interventions in order to learn about how change is possible. There is a large literature on speculative design, but here we focus on an example that brings together homes, social science and design approaches, by discussing the work of the STS (science and technology studies)-oriented sociologist Mike Michael's collaboration with the speculative designer Bill Gaver. Also in relation to developing new ways of thinking about energy demand in homes, Michael and Gaver's work uses a form of speculative design, whereby, Michael describes: 'Users are invited through various means such as cultural probes and ethnographic visits to generate material (say, views on the aesthetics of a dwelling's energy use, or idle doodles while talking on the phone, or photographs of a home's spiritual centre) which are combined with other materials (design history, recent media reports, online discussions and so on)' (2016: 106). The designers then create artefacts based on these materials which are 'a-functional' and 'ambiguous, and playful in ways that surprise the user, test their expectations, and enable unforeseen ways of thinking about the issues at stake' (2016: 106). This approach was mobilized in home environments. From the perspective that the home is a specific type of context for ethnography and design, it is relevant to consider how its particular affordances participate in how both practices can play out. Michael describes two examples of artefacts that were created and left in participants' homes, accounting for the effects these did (or did not) have on the speculative modes of the participants. In these research experiments speculative probes, made for and inserted into everyday life in the home (like other (supposedly) functional objects such as energy metres (see Strengers 2013) or washing machines (see Pink and Astari 2015) that are often not used as intended), were engaged with contextual and contingent ways, which illuminates as much about life in homes as it has the potential to bring about change.

Our proposal is for an interdisciplinary relationship between design and ethnography that is theoretically dialogic, attends to the sensory and digital environments of everyday life, follows the anthropological principle of reflexivity and is ethically engaged with people as they live in and explore their lives as research *participants*. This, we propose, is a condition for and outcome of the contemporary contexts of 'home' that design and intervention is developed for/in. As we outline in Chapter 5, approaches that take concepts such as practices and that use probes and forms of speculative inquiry offer useful starting points for researching the home through design and ethnography. However, in the spirit of approaching our field of research and intervention through concepts that have emerged from it, this book is structured around three concepts – temporalities, environments and activity. Each of these, as we explain in the following three chapters, informed but also emerged as re-crafted from our research into everyday life with digital media and energy, as key ways to view life in the home. Here we engage these as guiding concepts for understanding and intervening in homes. We invite readers to engage with them with the same openness that we present them, as malleable concepts, which might change or be refigured, disappear or be added to.

What is home?

The study of home and the processes, things and human activities that constitute it have a long history across anthropology, design research, geography, human–computer interaction (HCI), sociology, science and technology studies (STS) and cultural studies. Home is likewise a site for safety, social work and health research. To address the question of 'what are' the homes that might be researched, designed or might become sites for design interventions, we critically review recent disciplinary framings of home and how they help us to understand, for instance: the sensory and digital/mediated home; the politics and power dynamics of home, and the importance of studying everyday life in the home beyond its meaning as a site of 'domestication', 'comfort' and material culture; the notion of the smart home; and the home as a site of danger/safety, oppression and exclusion.

Definitions of home are broad and do not necessarily refer to home as a house, or fixed dwelling place that is inhabited by a family or other social unit household. Critical scholars have challenged this dominant definition (e.g. Dawson and Rapport 2001) to show how home might be a feeling, or a configuration of relationships and things. Such studies have referred to the situation of migrants and refugees, demonstrating that sensations of feeling 'at home' may be generated in localities distant from one's place of origin, through material culture, and memory objects (see also Pink and Postill 2016). This work questions how home might be constituted in contexts where housing is a problem or a lack, and in ways that suggest we need to look beyond materiality and architecture. Simultaneously the work we discuss here, which *does* centre on the house as home, enables us to also reflect on questions relating to the role of design in the making of intangible elements of home, in relation to migration, and other forms of displacement. We return to this in the concluding chapter, and acknowledge that the implication of the discussions to follow in this book is that future work should focus more on questions of how participatory design ethnography interventions might intervene productively in making homes in such situations.

However our work in this book is limited to homes that are made and experienced in the material form of a house and household of some kind. This might include, as discussed in earlier work, people living alone, in shared houses (Pink 2004), and older people (Burrows, Mitchell and Nicollle 2011; Lilley, Bhamra, Haines and Mitchell 2010). Home and the ways in which people live in houses are also culturally specific. Between the authors we have done research about homes in the United Kingdom, Spain, Indonesia and Australia and Romania. Likewise anthropologists and human geographers have shown how houses, homes and their meanings emerge across a wide range of contexts. For example the anthropologically influenced material culture studies-oriented work of Danny Miller (1988, 2001, 2008) and Alison Clarke (e.g. Clarke 2001, 2009) has had a focus on homes in the United Kingdom, while Pauline Garvey's work has been focused in Sweden (Garvey 2001, 2010), and that of Horst on digital media and everyday life in the home in the United States (Horst 2012), as well as with return migrant retirees in Jamaica (Horst 2008, 2009, 2011), and more recently Mikkel Bille's research engages with light and home in Lebanon and Denmark (Bille 2015a,b, 2017), yet also recognizes the future focus on design.

The contribution of human geographers to understanding home has created powerful accounts of the gendered politics of home and has highlighted the problematic nature of assumptions that home or house is necessarily a site of harmony. Feminist geographers such as Alison Blunt and Robyn Dowling, and Katherine Brickell have proposed a critical revision to how home and domestic life are understood, emphasizing how vulnerability and domestic violence (particularly for women) are part of domestic life that researchers need to attend to (Blunt and Dowling 2007; Brickell 2011, 2014). Brickell has called for attention to what she calls 'home unmaking' (2012: 262), whereby she proposes that

analytical approaches to the study of domestic life should not just be founded on the productive making of home life but also on moments and periods of discordance that also form part of household development. More specifically, while friction and negotiation have arguably become co-opted into the taken-for granted nature of 'intact' marital life, the significance of marital dissolution warrants more serious consideration. (Brickell 2012: 263)

This approach fits with our proposal that the home needs to be understood as an ongoingly changing configuration of people, things and processes. Yet we would not want to de-emphasize that studying home still very often involves research with families, including nontraditional family forms as well as intergenerational families and relationships (Hjorth et al. 2016), and that moreover design research in homes, in our experience, has indeed tended not to attend extensively to the idea of home as a site of conflict.

Home is, moreover, more than a site of family or intimate sociality in other ways. Homes are also workplaces, for people who work from home, for domestic workers who might be at risk of exploitation (Pratt 1999; Law 2001) and for those who deliver services, such as health care, deliveries (Pink et al. 2015) or social work (Ferguson 2008, 2009, 2010) in other people's homes. Blunt and Varley have suggested that 'ideas of home' here may 'invoke a sense of place, belonging or alienation that is intimately tied to a sense of self' (2004: 3). As Pink, Morgan and Dainty (2015) have argued, the ambiguity of home being a work and home place simultaneously is navigated by people who work in other people's homes in contingent ways. This is equally important to consider in relation to the home as a site for design, since homes are made – or 'unmade' – not only by family members or other intimate socialities but also through the mundane and sometimes more distant relations with others. These literatures call on us to attend to the politics of 'domestic geographies', and to how services and visitors to the home are implicated in its changing configurations. However they also bring our attention to situations where other family members play roles in ensuring that new home technologies are incorporated. For example, Alison Burrows and Val Mitchell's work on how older adults set up and begin using technology in the home in relation to 'the out of the box experience' highlighted how older adults tended to depend on others – often younger family members – to choose, set up and learn how to use technologies brought into the home. This on the one hand was part of the social benefits of integrating with others and was sometimes even a way of providing a role for others in their lives (an opportunity to help), while on the other being due to a need to gain help (Burrows, Mitchell and Nicole 2016). When added to the conventional questions raised by material culture studies, HCI and media studies approaches to home, these are significant questions for considering the home as a site of/for design, since making and unmaking (which can also be part of the same process) are implied in the activities of ordinary people as everyday designers. As Dourish and Bell (2011) have also highlighted, such issues are infrequently accounted for in design approaches to the home.

Finally, media technologies, content and communication are implicated and entangled with everyday life in the home. Scholars and researchers working across anthropology and (now digital) media studies have an established trajectory of debate in this area. This is embodied in earlier work on domestic technologies (e.g. Silverstone and Hirsch 1992; Morley 2000) and what was referred to as their 'domestication' or their appropriation, and in the 'moral economy' of the home (see Horst 2012 for a recent discussion of these perspectives). It is also characterized by a non-media-centric approach to media (Morley 2009; Moores 2012; Couldry 2012), or a non-digital-centric approach to digital media and technologies (Pink, Horst et al. 2016). The idea that the home now needs to be understood as a domain where the online and offline are intricately related (Horst 2012) is increasingly established as an inevitable element of research into everyday life in the home, and as argued elsewhere (Pink, Leder Mackley et al. 2016), it enables us to think of the home and how life is lived through it in relation to a concept of 'digital materiality'. Such an approach, in the context of design ethnography research, seeks to understand digital media and technologies by way of their situatedness in other aspects of everyday life. Examples of such an approach are developed by Pink and Leder Mackley (2013) and Pink, Leder Mackley and Moroşanu's (2015) discussions of how media technologies and content form an experiential presence in the home, which is sensed and becomes part of the everyday atmospheres through which homes are experienced and become meaningful. Other work shows how homes are sites for ambient digital play (Pink, Hjorth et al. 2017) and where intergenerational family relationships are played out through digital and social media. Obscured by the experience of such digital material environments of home are the code and data that participate in how homes are constituted. Homes are one of the sites that geographers Rob Kitchin and Martin Dodge discuss in relation to how 'code/spaces should be understood and conceptualised as relational and emergent spaces in which software frames the unfolding but does not determine it' (2011: 74). Kitchin and Dodge audit the ways and extents to which (digitally) coded objects are mobilized in three different types of home. In doing so they identify implications for how life in homes might emerge in relation to automated management systems they associate with a code-dominated world. They suggest that 'coded objects alter the material, social, and spatial relations of the home in new ways; they offer members of households new affordances to undertake domestic living differently' (2011: 174) and that varied types of 'control by code' will be mobilized in homes so that 'the home, previously seen as a sanctuary from an overdetermined and regulated world, becomes open to forms of automated management' (2011: 176). Yet Kitchin and Dodge do not predict a smooth transition to a smart home future but envision a future based on their understanding that: 'How coded objects beckon space into being is not deterministic, rather it is contingent and relational'. In this future, 'The spatiality of different homes, even if they were materially identical, would vary substantially because the technologies would be used in different ways, within varying contexts' (2011: 179).

The contingencies of the everyday tend to foil the ambitions of the technologically possible visions that Kitchin and Dodge (2011) portray in their critical analysis of code (as they acknowledge but do not investigate ethnographically), and that are discussed by Yolande Strengers (2016) in her critical account of the smart home. As these works, and our own research into digital technologies in homes indicate, the smart home is a concept and a technological possibility, yet it will only be realized as it is lived by real people in the messy and contingent flow of real everyday lives. Such issues have also been raised in the HCI literature (Swan, Taylor and Harper 2008; Taylor et al. 2007). As Taylor et al. have pointed out, 'It is people who imbue their homes with intelligence by continually weaving together things in their physical worlds with their everyday routines and distinct social arrangements' (2007). This is moreover why we argue that before even considering the smart home, we need to generate and mobilize a series of more fundamental understandings of what home is and can be, through ethnography and design. As Strengers also emphasizes, in her critical account of the smart home, it is 'not what people think about energy or how they "use" smart home technologies, but how they negotiate everyday living – doing the laundry, cooking dinner, running the air-conditioner – and how these dynamics are disrupted or transformed through smart home technologies' (2016: 63) that matter. Likewise, in this book we attend to questions of how everyday life is lived in the home, and how ethnographic and design research and interventions might best be implicated in this. We are, inevitably, concerned with the future home, or at least with the future orientation of design for homes, always with an eye to the digital and to the technologically possible. Yet we emphasize that the possible is not the future but only an indication of something that could be part of it. The idea that digital technologies should be accounted for creates both a persuasive argument and a powerful challenge for the design of the future home, and for the design of homes as we ongoingly move on into our futures. However this does not necessarily lead us to the conclusion that we need to design smart homes. We return to this in the concluding chapter to this book.

A design ethnography approach to the home

Design and ethnography are large fields of practice. We do not attempt to cover their diversity but rather to focus on their applications in homes. To preface the discussion in the following chapters, we examine the particularities of the home as a site for both practices; we then bring together ideas from the previous sections of this chapter to define everyday life in the home as a design question and a social science question.

Ethnography is a research practice used across a range of qualitative social science disciplines, as well as by designers. Each use is inflected by the critical demands of disciplines, the needs of research questions and the various other ways of knowing, learning, documenting and sharing it might come up against. It has been defined as minimally

> iterative-inductive research (that evolves in design through the study), drawing on a family of methods, involving direct and sustained contact with human agents, within the context of their daily lives (and cultures), watching what happens, listening to what is said, asking questions, and producing a richly written account that respects the irreducibility of human experience, that acknowledges the role of theory as well as the researcher's own role and that views humans as part object/part subject. (O'Reilly 2005: 3)

However, across disciplines ethnographic practice also becomes shaped by new technological and theoretical '*turns*' and moves (Pink 2015) – hence approaches that have been called *Virtual Ethnography* (Hines 2000), *Visual Ethnography* (Pink 2001, 2007, 2013), *Netnography* (Kozinets 2011) or *Sensory Ethnography* (Pink 2009, 2015). We discuss design ethnographic research methods in the home in Chapter 5; however, before considering the home as a site for ethnography as we do in Chapters 2–4, we emphasize that the home has some special characteristics that distinguish it from conventional long-term ethnographic fieldwork sites that are often associated with anthropological research. As has been pointed out by Danny Miller (2001), and reinforced in our own experience (Pink 2004; Pink and Leder Mackley 2012), 'Ethnographers working in such environments often respond by carrying out their researches in very different situation from traditional ethnography. Usually they do not live with a family, but visit' (Miller 2001: 3). Miller and the contributors to his *Home Possessions* volume (Miller 2001) demonstrate such visit-based ethnographies as they were undertaken across a range of countries including Norway (Garvey 2001), Romania (Drazin 2001), Canada (Marcoux 2001), Japan (Daniels 2001) and the United Kingdom (Clarke 2001; Hecht 2001). More recently methods for doing ethnographies in home have become increasingly experimental (Moroşanu 2016), interdisciplinary (Osz 2016) and design-oriented (Pink, Leder Mackley et al. 2016). This is partly a response to the shorter timescales involved in applied and intervention-oriented research. In order not to be excessively intrusive, 'short-term' methods (Pink and Morgan 2014) and the creation of intensive encounters, using video (Pink and Leder Mackley 2014) or photography, in place of longer-term hanging around (e.g. Horst 2006, 2011), can also be suited to researching with people in homes. Ethnographies of homes thus involve particular bundles of qualitative methods, used as appropriate in relation to particular circumstances and contingencies of people and place.

While for designers seeing the home as an active site for change-making is not novel or challenging, this book also makes a specific argument in this vein towards the social sciences. The home is a key site of everyday life, and a context where significant interventions towards achieving important goals – such as sustainable futures, gender-equitable ways of living – might be focused. The social sciences and humanities have traditionally been rather good at studying the home, pointing out the inequalities of domestic life, the ways that material cultures are implicated in the making of everyday life in the home, and arguing for attention to the more problematic, violent and oppressive aspects of home. Yet there are increasing calls for the social sciences and humanities to be more active in the world, to come closer than the traditional critical distance created by their analyses has permitted, and to produce an engaged, applied scholarship. Bringing together the ways of knowing (about) and being in the world that have emerged in these disciplines with design research, scholarship and practice creates a route to a new form of engaged scholarship and practice, which can be used to seek to address precisely the problems that the social sciences and humanities have been so good at identifying and producing critical literatures on, but have not sought to resolve through practical action. *Making Homes* is a call for us to continue to go beyond this state of play, and to do so by forging relationships and new ways of working between social and design disciplines, through the bringing together of ethnography and design practice.

The book

To conclude this introduction we outline the sequence, organization and argument of the following chapters.

The next three chapters of this book – Chapters 2–4 – focus on three key conceptual themes concerning researching and designing for homes and everyday life in homes: temporalities, environments, and activity and movement. Each theme represents a set of engagements between research and design in and about homes and theoretical understandings. They are built on our collective extensive experience of working with participants in their homes over a number of projects over the last fifteen or so years – as anthropologists, media scholars and design researchers – and have been refined through our collaborative work over the last five or so years. The three themes of temporalities, environments, and activity and movement are also significant themes in contemporary academic debates. Each chapter is prefaced by a discussion of the relevance of each respective theme, how it has developed and how it can help us to (re) think the home as a site for ethnography and design. Together however they offer us three complementary – and indeed inseparable – visions of the home and everyday life in it. These all take home as an open place and concept and respectively acknowledge how it is ongoingly changing, its complexity as a place made up of things and processes of different qualities and affordances, and its dynamism as a site that these things and processes are continually passing through or moving around in.

Chapter 5 broaches the question of how we might go about researching the home as an open and ongoingly moving and changing place. In this chapter we present a series of methods that have been developed with this challenge in mind. There, we do not intend to offer methods 'on the peg' that can be taken off and applied in exactly the same way elsewhere. Rather, our aim is to set out a series of methodological templates and tested techniques that might be adapted and planted to grow further in new projects. The principles behind these methods are focused on themes of reflexivity, adaptability, visual, digital and sensory engagements with participants; collaboration with participants; and the broad principle of doing ethnography *with* and not about people. The methods draw on traditions in anthropology, design, documentary film, arts practice and crafts, and in bringing them together, we argue, for an interdisciplinary approach to making methods.

Finally, in Chapter 6 we sum up the implications for future research and design agendas that are opened up by a design ethnography approach to the home. These moves are significant for both social science and design research. We argue that the future orientation of design requires social science theory to critically interrogate the future as a concept, and to acknowledge how the temporalities these investigations imply might require us to rethink how we understand the home as a temporal environment.

2

Temporalities

This chapter examines the temporalities of ethnography, design and everyday life with specific reference to how these are articulated and lived out through research, design and everyday life in the home. We take a human-focused approach to temporality, and therefore we explore ways of being in everyday life (as well as in ethnographic and design practice), which are characterized by the capacity to imagine a world where different degrees of past, present and future exist. For the moment, in taking that approach we ask readers to suspend thoughts of what else in the world might be involved in making temporalities of home. We engage with such questions in the following chapter by examining environments of home and situating human experience, memories and imagination in relation to the technologies, digital materialities and sensoriality of home.

We focus on how present- and future-oriented logics that are part of cultures and societies emerge in the contexts of ethnography, design and everyday life engagements with homes. It is relevant to attend to temporality and the issues that it raises in these three domains because a solid understanding of temporalities, what they are, and how they work, is fundamental to practices of change-making. Change-making is an inevitably future-oriented activity or imaginary and to be able to engage with it in an informed way we need to be able to understand what 'future' can mean, where it might be situated, where it might be related to the present, and what the politics of our engagements with it imply.

In the following sections we explore further the temporalities at play in anthropological ethnographic practice, in the everyday lives of people as they live and improvise in their homes, and as they have been understood in design anthropology. We explore the consequences of consolidating these temporalities of ethnography and of everyday life in the home, for creating a new understanding of how past-present-future can figure in interventions for change, and for design ethnography in the home.

Interrogating the temporalities of ethnography

While design and ethnography are increasingly being brought together in highly productive ways, there have also been various difficulties associated with past attempts to achieve this. Jamer Hunt has suggested that one explanation for this is related to their different approaches to temporality since 'these two practices – design and ethnography – represent dramatically different orientations toward change and time. More specifically, each practice configures its methods in relation to slightly incommensurable temporal frameworks, producing a disjuncture between them that is both revealing and potentially generative of new directions' (Hunt 2010: 34). Here we examine these issues further in the context of researching and designing in homes, to point to how a more productive and generative relationship between the temporalities of anthropology and design might be developed through attention to the temporalities of home and the everyday.

Conventional anthropological ethnography and its relationship to design is reflected accurately in the way that Hunt sums up the difference. He writes of an approach to ethnography that 'attempts to illuminate the present by interrogating its (recent) past' using methods that are 'observational, descriptive, analytical, and interpretive', noting that 'ethnography is rarely projective; it does not speculate on what might happen next. Its focus is the present, built upon a series of past "present" moments' (2010: 35). This description definitely corresponds with conventional anthropological ethnography and suits the comparison with design that Hunt goes on to make. We question its ongoing relevance as a definition of contemporary ethnography for reasons outlined further below. However as a foil to a productive relationship with design, the characterization works well, since Hunt describes 'design, on the other hand, … [as] … a practice of material and immaterial making, ... its mode of being-in-the-world is generative, speculative, and transformational'. Therefore while he sees ethnographers as fixed on the past-present, he writes that 'a designer must project forward into a potential future to launch an artifact that will, if all goes right, transform a near present and rewrite our future' (Hunt 2010: 35).

Hunt is right that conventional anthropological ethnography has been something of a misfit with design and intervention, yet his description caricatures ethnography in the form that is advocated by the more traditional anthropologists. The focus on the present/past in anthropology has an important critical history in the discipline, and indeed there is a strong (and often correct) conviction among anthropologists that this is also an *ethical stance*. To briefly summarize, ethnographic research was originally written into what was referred to as the 'ethnographic present'; this meant that descriptions of other people, cultures or societies were written as if they were crystallized in a moment in the present. However in the 1980s a critical body of literature led by the anthropologist, Johannes Fabian, began to problematize this fixing of the ethnographic 'other' in a timeless present. Representing other people(s) as unchanging was seen as problematically objectifying, disrespectful and was moreover empirically neglectful of the reality that people, cultures and societies are ongoingly changing. The response to this critique has meant that since then, most ethnographers, and in particular anthropological ethnographers, are careful to write their ethnographies about things that had happened, that is to situate them in the past, to represent the things that they had been told or had observed as being things that had happened in that particular past moment and in relation to particular configurations of things, persons and circumstances. The reflexive stance taken by what has been called the 'writing culture' debate embodies much of this work (see Clifford and Marcus 1986) and has had an enduring influence.

However, by focusing on this aspect of anthropology, Hunt does not account for the growth of creative and alternative methods in anthropology, and more broadly across interdisciplinary ethnographic practice, but only accounts for the descriptive and past-focused stance. He also does not account for the critical, interrogatory and sometimes playful accounts of ethnographic filmmaking, public anthropology and applied anthropology, which are equally reflexive and indeed also adopt the past-focused respect for what has already happened, but that are *also* orientated towards making a series of interventions in the world. Indeed, by focusing on the most conservative end of anthropology in order to demonstrate the differences between ethnography and design, and the ways in which their temporalities do not meet, Hunt shows up the challenges, but in doing so unfortunately caricatures anthropology at only one of its extremes. This is because, at the other end of anthropology – the *applied, public* and *interventional* end of the discipline – which was for a long period of time rejected as not being real scholarship (see for example Wright 2005; Mills 2005) by the anthropological establishment, there have already been a series of innovations that make ethnography very ready to engage with design. These include developments in applied visual anthropology (see Pink 2007) and where visual anthropology practice has long since been connected to design anthropology (e.g. Sperschneider 2007), corporate anthropology (Cefkin 2009), the inventive methods movement in sociology (Lury and Wakeford 2012), what have been called 'irregular ethnographies' (O'Dell and Willim 2011) and future anthropologies techniques (Salazar, Pink, Irving and Sjoberg 2017). Such approaches to ethnography in common tend to use methods that are more experimental and that are orientated towards public and applied interventions in the world (see Pink et al. 2013).

Moreover, new methodological approaches to conducting specifically future-oriented ethnographies are emerging. These include ethnographies of the possible, speculative ethnography and documentary, and experimental and fiction-based techniques (e.g. Halse 2013; Akama and Pink 2015; Salazar et al. 2017; Pink and Salazar 2017). We discuss such methods specifically in relation to researching the home in Chapter 5. By making a connection with the future orientation of design, applied ethnographic practice is better able to contribute to the change-making and future-making interventions in the world that applied ethnographers have already been participating in or seeking to make. The home is no less a site for such processes to begin.

Applied ethnographic practice in social science more generally, where ethnographers seek to understand the logics and dynamics of and to contribute to and participate in change-making and intervention, is increasingly supported by a series of theoretical and methodological contributions (Pink, Fors and O'Dell 2017). The relationship of applied ethnography to theory is twofold. On the one hand, ideally, and specifically in the model we are advocating, applied ethnography is developed in dialogue with theoretical debates and contributes to these debates. Yet on the other hand, there are particular theoretical perspectives that might be attached to applied ethnography, that distinguish it from conventional academic scholarship and practice in the social sciences. The theoretical arguments and debates that support research and scholarship in this field are important to account for because if we wish to participate in change or future-making as social scientists, we need to critically interrogate the field in which we wish to practice, to understand how it is constituted, experienced and conceptualized by others. This means problematizing and critically interrogating the concept of future itself, as it is present in society, in the contexts in which we research and in ethnographic practice itself, and also how it is likewise constituted, activated and imagined in design practice. It also entails taking a reflexive stance towards our own practice as ethnographers and as designers, and applying the same principles to analysing how we use our methods and approaches to make and imagine futures, that we apply to studying how participants in our research do so.

A starting point for reassessing how we might conceptualize the relevance of temporality for applied research is therefore supported by the growing interest across social science, humanities and design disciplines in rethinking how we conceptualize time, and in particular it has enabled us to think about futures in relation to the present, the past, the imagination and their politics in new ways. This includes literatures about the sociology of time (Adam and Groove 2007), the sociology of expectations (Brown and Michael 2003), anthropologies of the future (see Pink and Salazar 2017), and of imagination (Sneath et al. 2009) or anticipatory geographies (Anderson 2010). Yet more recently new ways of thinking about temporality in ethnography are emerging, for example in the development of the 'anthropology of the future', 'ethnographies of the possible' (Halse 2013), and the exploration of techniques for researching the future (Salazar et al. 2017), which enable ethnography to develop a future orientation. Recent writings on the temporality of ethnography have also developed new ways of thinking about the temporality of the ethnographic process itself, through a theory of ethnographic place (Pink 2014), which encompasses the future as well as the past-present of ethnographies.

Little of this literature has to date specifically referred to researching ethnographic futures related to home. Nevertheless, a range of such future-oriented modes can be identified as being embedded in the ways that everyday life in the home is played out. Some of these can be seen as part of everyday perceptual ways of knowing, learning, imagining and anticipating how we engage with other people and environments. Others are more evidently bound up with societal, institutional and regulatory trends. For instance as part of financial and capital movements which emerge with the future forecasting of economics, as part of the anticipatory modes of planning (Abram 2017) and building regulation, and through the ways in which designers themselves imagine smart home futures. Empirically, temporality has also become an increasing focus across fields that have direct relevance for researching and intervention in homes, in media studies (Keightly 2012), in Pink's notion of the 'project' of home (Pink 2004) or the idea that homes have elements of 'incompletion' (Horst 2006), in anthropologies of planning (e.g. Horst 2008; Abram 2017), and in studying how homes are also part of projects of imagining (Horst 2011). Such work has also specifically attended to how digital technologies are implicated in temporalities of home, with particular interest in future homes. This is found in sociological and science and technology studies (STS) through a focus on smart homes and automation in the home (Strengers 2013, 2016), in work that crosses anthropology and HCI, where Dourish and Bell (2011) have critically explored the implications of a revised view of ubiquitous computing for digital futures in the home, and in our own work on digital interventions in homes (Pink, Leder Mackely et al. 2016). Collectively these works indicate that to think of the home should not to be to imagine a site that is fixed in the present or only understandable in relation to the past. Rather, we need to account for how home is already always situated in the temporalities of people, organizations and discourses, in ways that incorporate a future orientation, *but* whereby the modes of future and the experiences associated with them will vary.

This, we argue is key to understanding the possibilities of a design ethnography approach to the home: to be effective, such an approach cannot be separated out from the temporalities and notions of futures through which people *live out* and experience their everyday lives in their homes.

Temporalities of homes

If we are to be able to develop change or future-making interventions with people through their everyday lives in their homes, we need to understand how they experience and give meaning to the temporalities of their lives and the digital, material and sensory environments in which they live. We need to be able to account for the future-oriented perceptions and actions of participants in ethnographic and design projects, rather than to simply see them as subjects to whom future-oriented research and design approaches will be applied. Indeed, we must consider how ethnographic and design research and practice encounter, and might become entangled with, participants' future orientations in beneficial ways.

In this section we examine a set of examples of how temporalities of home are constituted by ordinary people as they live out and imagine their lives at home, as exemplified through the existing literature as well as our own research. These are: the 'project' of home; routines and rhythms of everyday life; moments of transition in the home, such as at bedtime; uses of 'time', timers, clocks and other time-based technologies; anticipatory near-future modes of temporality in the home; and seasonality and weather. The examples are drawn from our own and other researchers' ethnographies. They are intended as examples of what can be found, rather than as a template or model for what will always be found, simply because ethnography and design involves encountering the specific. However simultaneously we recommend that the concepts and insights discussed here might be taken forward as a set of principles through which to guide studies of and interventions into futures in everyday life in homes. Because they are developed ethnographically, based on culturally specific contexts, they will not necessarily be universally applicable, but may be used to provoke research and analytical questions across different research contexts.

Moreover, institutional, governmental and regulatory temporalities of home and the ways everyday life is lived in it are also at play and have an inevitable impact on how the home is experienced, constituted and lived. These include the temporalities of the payment of bills, rent, mortgages, garbage collection and other public and private services to the home. However they also include the anticipatory modes of neo-liberal planning regimes (Abram 2017) and their ability to determine aspects of the materiality and experience of home (or to be resisted) (see also Gunn and Clausen 2013: 167 for mention of regulation). The risk averse and heritage-focused protection and preventative logics of buildings planning approval for domestic homes, for instance, dictate the width and height of certain structures and the placements of doors and windows. These work, in different ways, towards the future of the home, as safe and as historic, yet they often have different logics to do-it-yourself (DIY) and everyday design practices.

The project of home

The idea that home, or the making of homes can be seen as a 'project' which is continually ongoing (Pink 2004), indicates that homes are usually continually being made or remade in a number of material and sensory ways. In UK contexts in ethnographic research, often the home was presented in this way, so that when we toured and video recorded homes with participants, and they showed us how they lived in them, as pointed out elsewhere 'the present which was encountered in the video tour of the home was only presentable to us as researchers when accompanied by accounts of the past and visions of the future and a sense of what the home would feel like in the future' (Pink et al. 2015). In design research this temporality of home is equally relevant. For example, Mallaband, Haines and Mitchell discuss how in another interdisciplinary energy-focused project 'Consumer Appealing Low Energy technologies for Building REtrofitting' (CALEBRE), they used a bespoke participatory design tool to construct with householders a timeline of their home around which they told us their home improvement stories (Mallaband et al. 2013). Equally as Pauline Garvey's research into Swedish IKEA stores and with householders as consumers demonstrates, one can think of the way that IKEA goods are marketed as forms of 'inspiration' that participate in such processes of making homes through domestic design artefacts (Garvey 2010).

Theoretically we can interpret these changes through a processual theory whereby we might understand the world as continually being made and changing, and homes likewise as having porous material, sensory and digital boundaries, which mean that they are not static entities but shifting and contingent configurations of things and processes. Indeed when we set participants' understandings of the home within the context of a discussion of temporality, it becomes clear that past-present-future are closely intertwined in people's projects of home. These research insights enable us to see how participants' understandings of their realities and the possibilities for action they have within them can be situated through the idea of ongoing change, but that their future imaginaries for their homes might be located in a range of different ways in relation to the present, and in relation to whether or not their realization is realistic or not.

In some cases as Pink's earlier research with UK and Spanish participants revealed, the home is seen as 'incomplete' (2004: 57) or unfinished. Pink argued that 'as a forever incomplete project home is never completely realised materially, but instead exists partially in one's imagination as a series of constantly developing dreams or plans' (2004: 58). This interpretation of how participants in research understood their homes has been consistent across different research projects and cultural contexts in the United Kingdom, Spain and Indonesia (e.g. Pink 2004; Pink et al. 2015; Pink and Astari 2015). In some cases these changes over time referred to when a family might expand, or when participants would become older and need the home to be differently arranged. In other earlier examples we can see how the project of home is one of the imagination, that might never happen or that involves materializing aspirations in ways that may be incomplete. Moreover while these tendencies play out differently in different cultural and national contexts, the future consistently shows up as part of how people experience homes. For instance, Alison Clarke discussed how one of the participants in her research projects about London homes talked of changes she wished to make to her home, which never came about. In this example Clarke goes into some detail about how the participant maintained a vision of her future home, but at the same time could cite a range of reasons why it did not materialize (Clarke 2001). Another example is demonstrated by Heather Horst's research with Jamaican returnee migrants from the United Kingdom. Horst (2006) has argued that 'returnees' construction and organization of the home, and in turn the household, expresses a tension between completion and incompletion, a tension fundamentally linked to being and becoming a returned resident'. Here, Horst shows that while the completion of the home is associated with the completion of a person's identity as a returned migrant, even so there is an element of incompletion involved since there is always work to be done on the home and there are children's visits to await.

While the case discussed by Horst is inextricable from the specifics of the Jamaican migrant trajectory, such future-oriented imaginaries of home are often seen as bound up with forms of capitalist consumption. For instance, Pauline Garvey, who has undertaken ethnographic research on IKEA and homes in Sweden and Ireland, sees IKEA as the 'materialization of inspiration' (Garvey 2010: 142), where 'inspiration … does not necessarily imply transformation but rather gives name to a contemplation of possibilities' (Garvey 2010: 143). Businesses such as IKEA might help people to contemplate the possible. However it is likely that this is related to already existing (although culturally specific) tendencies to imagine possible domestic materialities and sensations. This proposal invites us to think of the home as always in process, yet at the same time always imagined into a possible future, which goes beyond that actuality and materiality of the tangible changes that are already being made or experienced.

The sometimes dramatic and imaginative ways in which people imagine, anticipate, plan to alter, or fantasize about, changing or making their homes simultaneously form part of how people live in their homes. Sometimes these are concrete and material processes that are in fact in progress – such as the home alteration project we outline below. In other cases, however, they may be projects that are never realized, or simply ways of feeling what it might be like if things were different when walking through the home. In common these imagined future homes all generate the notion of the home as a project and the *projection* of the home into the future tense when showing and talking about it.

To illustrate how this might happen in practice, we draw on the example of the Ashton family. Elsewhere, we have described how this family, which participated in our LEEDR project, was in the process of making alterations to their home.

> The Ashtons' home was ongoingly designed through their intentional and continuing engagement with home improvement and DIY (Do it Yourself) activities. This process, in ways similar to other participants' stories, lent the way they spoke of and showed the home a future orientation. Since moving in, the family had made extensive structural, spatial and sensory changes to the house. It was modernized, enlarged and 'brightened up'. During the video tour of their home they explained how the front door and main stairs were moved and the kitchen extended to double its size. They contracted a builder for the extension and larger works, however the walls, flooring, tiling, skirting boards, some upholstering and décor that were seen and recorded on video, were created through the embodied labor of DIY and Barbara's creative and practical skills. This changed the surfaces, textures and feel of home, for instance through pulling up carpets to reveal original flooring. Yet the home was ongoing; they were sure to tell us that a separate toilet and sink unit had just been completed, and the shower room, described as 'like a shower in a cupboard, that leaks' would be next. (Pink, Leder Mackley and Moroşanu 2015)

The idea that the home is on a trajectory of change is also represented in other cultural contexts, as shown in the film *Laundry Lives* (Pink and Astari 2015). In this project, while participants did not tend to qualify their present homes through the tense of what they would be like in the future, the idea of the home in progress was also present. Indonesian research participants, when asked about their futures, reflected in part on how they would like their homes to be in the future. Thus they were also seeing their homes as projects, which might change in their material, technological and social configurations in the future. For example in some cases such visions of the near and far future might be told in relation to domestic technologies, but always in relation to the immediate existing experience of participants. For example, one *Laundry Lives* participant, a student and son of another participant, imagined a future home where

FIGURE 2.1 AND **2.2** *Lia imagined a future home where she would get a machine that everything came out of neat, while Nur's older son, a student, imagined one where robots would serve humans. Both drew on their immediate knowledge and experience to anticipate these futures. Indeed when people are asked to discuss what is next, they will inevitably draw on what they already know and experience. In Chapter 5, we discuss how speculative research techniques can enable departures from this. © Sarah Pink and Nadia Astari 2015.*

humans were served by robots, while another hoped that she would have a dishwasher next. Everyday life ways of thinking about what might be next tend to be situated in such a way, in terms of personal and cultural experience. They are demonstrated well through intensive research with people in their homes.

Understanding the home as being in progress and ongoingly imagined in another alterity offers us a key insight into designing for and intervening in homes. It suggests that it involves designing for a project of making that already has a future orientation. The home, when presented to researchers, is always something that is *becoming*. Designing for the home means designing for a material, sensory and emotional environment that is aspirational and coming into being and that is not always articulated verbally but might be felt or imagined in more corporeal ways. We discuss techniques for researching corporeal or embodied knowing and imagining in the home in Chapter 5.

The routines and rhythms of everyday life: Transition moments

Above we discussed how the home is ongoingly made or imagined as a project, which might change or be changed over time (see also Pink 2012). The home is also continuously made and remade through the routines and rhythms of everyday life. Some of these routines make, unmake and then remake elements of everyday life in the home, like cleaning, cooking and tidying. They are smaller than the bigger renovation, or DIY projects of home that participants have discussed across different projects. However routines of remaking and renewal of the home also have a future orientation in that they are part the process of the ongoingness of home. They are part of the way in which we move forward through the world as we live out our everyday lives. In contrast to the *projects of home* discussed above, they do not involve a projected imaginary, but are more specifically involved in the planning and anticipation of what might happen next, in the preparation for ongoing activities and in the ordering and accomplishment of the everyday in such a way that enables things to continue *as if as normal*. However it would be a mistake to see this ongoingness and seeming renewal as a way of maintaining the home *as it is*. In fact, as our research has shown, the performance of everyday routines shifts over time, in various ways. It also involves improvisation, which we discuss further in the next section, and which means that routines might still be performed, but that the detail of the way they are played out might change. Such changes might seem insignificant if one was studying the persistence of routines. However when routines are performed slightly differently, this can shift, for instance, the amount of energy, water, food or other resources that is consumed during a routine or activity. We explain how these activities work towards the ongoing process by which we, through everyday life activities, both make and step over into our futures in mundane and sometimes unnoticed ways through a series of examples below. First, however, we discuss how the routines of everyday life in the home have been approached in existing literatures and the implications of this for understanding how everyday futures are made.

Routines and habits have formed a key topic in the social sciences (see Martens et al. 2014) and in particular have been seen as useful analytical units through which to explore everyday life in the home. As Martens et al. point out, this is part of a contemporary neo-liberal research agenda in which 'one reason why recent years have seen a growing international and cross-disciplinary interest in "practices" and the formation and salience of routines and habits is the connection with applied research contexts' where it has been engaged to examine fundamental sociocultural questions relating for instance to sustainability agendas, workplace health and safety and more generally, into policy-related questions with an emphasis on 'behaviour' and 'behavioural change' (Martens et al. 2014: 1–2). With reference to the home such agendas have been applied to a range of mundane domestic routines and activities associated with questions such as food safety, energy and water demand. With its inevitable future orientation towards change, we see how practices, routines and habits have to some extent become regarded as the objects of analysis and the objects for futures designs. However, as we emphasize below, routines, habits and practices are already ongoingly changing, and therefore are difficult to redesign without the collaboration of the everyday designers who are already involved in this process.

There are a range of examples of how the temporalities of home are constituted through the routines and rhythms of everyday life. Drawing from examples of our own research and other relevant existing work, we do not offer an ideal type model of what such routines and rhythms might do or look like, but instead show how, in principle, we might go about understanding the home as a temporal phenomenon and gain a sense of the dynamics of its future orientation through these forms of activity. For instance, when using the kitchen to cook, eating and then cleaning up to restore it to pretty much as it was before. Each time these processes are followed small changes will be made, improvisations to adapt to changing circumstances, which might or might not be thought out. Some examples of how everyday washing up and laundry routines are experienced are discussed elsewhere in Pink's *Situating Everyday Life* (2012). Everyday laundry routines also form the narrative of *Laundry Lives* (Pink and Astari 2015) documentary, where some women participants also describe how they play out their morning routines so that they can be free to spend the day focusing on their professional work. Here we can see how everyday domestic routines are organized in such a way that they support the women's professional activities, meaning that the accomplishment of the morning routine signifies being able to move on uninterrupted into the next stage of the day. As one participant, Lia, pointed out, if her washing machine did not fill up with water quickly, this would hold up her other activities.

Studying routines and rhythms of everyday life enables us to see how people are continually slipping over the edge of the present and into the future as their everyday lives proceed. This is important for us to acknowledge as ethnographers and designers because it is often in the moments in which this happens that people improvise, when they are faced with the contingencies of the other things and processes that surround them. At the moments they need to use what they already know, including guesswork and judgement to alter, adapt and appropriate what is around them in order to be able to carry on.

In different projects we are required to focus on different aspects and moments of everyday routines. For example in the projects discussed above, the authors were interested in particular clusters of activity, such as laundry, washing up and bathroom cleaning. They also understood these activities as happening in relation to and as entangled with other activities. In the LEEDR project, because we were particularly interested in energy demand and digital media use, we took as our starting point four moments in the temporal and practical structure and routine of everyday life which we had identified as being potentially interesting for understanding energy resource consumption and digital technology use in the home. These, we believed, would also therefore be key moments that would be important to understand when designing for change or making sustainability interventions in the home. They were going to bed and getting up in the morning, leaving the home to go out (usually to go to work), and arriving home (usually from work). Our hunch proved to be right, and in our analysis we paid particular attention to bedtime and morning routines, which stood out as relevant transition moments. We also found that with reference to energy demand, these provided a useful contrast to the more typical research focus on sets of identified activity (or 'practices') like media use, laundry or showering, given that when the transition routine became the unit of analysis, it was easier to situate these activities as having dispersed elements that were often entangled with other activity. Generally transition routines have been neglected in the existing literature in favour of those activities that are associated with forms of consumption – such as showering and laundry (e.g. see Shove 2003; Gran Hannsen 2007; Pink 2012). As we show when we discuss these in Chapter 4, these activities can be usefully studied as part of routines of movement, through the home.

Our work on transition routines among households in the United Kingdom revealed similar activities across households. This was not unexpected since we worked with a culturally specific sample. Indeed, similarly, morning routines were similar among Muslim Indonesian women who participated in *Laundry Lives* (Pink and Astari 2015), when women tended to rise early, pray, do domestic chores, including putting the laundry on, and prepare breakfast. Likewise a study of arrival at home routines undertaken in France, using first-person perspective camera technologies to record participants' arrivals, investigated what it was to feel 'at home' (Cordelois 2010: 461); this study, which was based on social psychology, found that participants' activities on arriving home were very consistent:

> Once inside their home, all subjects drop their bag and their coat or jacket. They all put their keys in a dedicated place, by convention. Those for whom the return was the last of the day, put on slippers or at least take off their shoes and stay in socks (82% of cases). One of the most surprising things we noticed is that all people who have just come home do the same thing: they look around, sometimes walk around the whole house or apartment. Explanations for this were, for example, 'I look to see what I have to do,' 'I check whether something has changed,' or 'I look to see if my place is like I want it to be' (Cordelois 2010: 452)

In our LEEDR project, the routines through which participants finally 'closed down' their homes at night commonly began with the last person who went to bed, starting this transition sitting on the sofa, watching TV in the living room, and involved switching, locking and checking activities. Good examples of this are given in videos 23, 28, 29 and 32 at www.energyanddigitalliving.com in the video archive, and the re-enactment methodology used to research this is discussed in Chapter 5. In these videos we see the participants following similar routes through their homes, which are familiar to them and performed daily (although never in exactly the same way every day). These routines brought together the key themes of our findings in the LEEDR project, since being part of the way atmospheres are constituted (discussed in Chapter 3) and because they were routines in movement (discussed in Chapter 4). As we see as the discussions in those chapters unfold, there we can see how the temporalities, atmospheres and movement through the home are bound together. With specific reference to their significance for understanding temporalities of home, transition routines between day and night enable a new phase in the cycle to come into being, they move the home on into its future in an explicit way, while remaining in synch with human experiences of tiredness, and changes outdoors, towards darkness, and street lighting. However, night-time routines are also future-oriented, and not simply about creating a close segment of the day/night cycle. Indeed they can also be seen as anticipatory routines in that they include elements of preparation for what is assumed to happen later, or the next day, in that they involve charging phones during the night, setting up machines to go on during the night (see below), and ensuring that everything is place so that household members can sleep and themselves be prepared for the next day (Pink and Leder Mackley 2013).

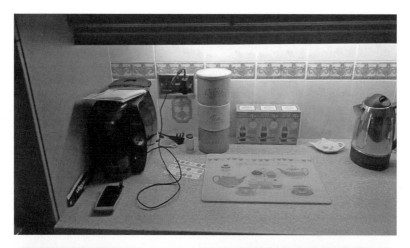

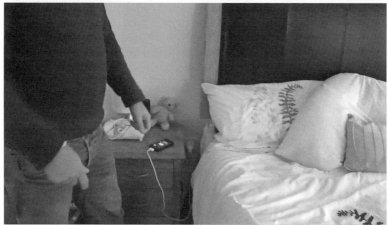

FIGURE 2.3 *Phones charging during the night.*

Timing

Another conceptualization of time at home is constituted through the use of the 'timer'. Timers are used for multiple purposes, most of which entailed participants semi-automating some aspects of their everyday life activities. Our own work has shown that they are used in relation to ways of ordering and organizing the structure of everyday (and night-time) activities, for achieving forms of automation, and indirectly as part of the process of creating atmospheres or particular sensory aesthetics of home. A common use of timers discussed in Pink's earlier research in UK homes, as well as in the LEEDR project, was on washing machines and dishwashers, so that these would go on during the night, to take advantage of cheaper energy costs. These were not necessarily isolated activities however, and, for instance, getting the washing machine ready for its night-time cycle for one participant coincided with feeding the cat, showing how the routine brought together a set of temporal activities. However such discussions also sometimes covered contingencies related to why a washing machine could not be left to go on via a timer. For example, Rhodes told us how she could not put her washing machine on a timer to go on at night because her son would be asleep in the room above (see Pink and Leder Mackley 2012). For others, it was left on at some risk; one family who used the washing machine timer at an almost nightly basis told us that they had to be careful not to overload the machine as it would sometimes cut out and 'trip' lights and other electrical gadgets on the same circuit.

Through our analysis of night-time routines, we learned that the use of timers for media technologies at bedtime enabled participants to create a bedtime atmosphere that would diminish as or when they went to sleep, without their having to intervene. This constituted a semi-automated process, in that they would switch on and listen to or watch their TV, radio or music, but they would also leave them to automatically turn off (see Pink and Leder Mackley 2012, 2013 for examples). In one of our online articles (Pink and Leder Mackley 2012) we include a video clip of Rhodes, who we noted above could not use her washing machine with a timer, due to everyday contingencies. Here Rhodes explained the process of using her TV on a timer and discussed the chain of contingencies through which this happened. Indeed such timers need not exactly be ticking to the minute, but rather other technologies were sometimes used as timers, or as markers of particular temporal sequences which participants knew would automatically end. For instance in one family each child would go to bed listening to music, while they drifted off to sleep. Because the music played always had a temporality to it, would last for a known period of time, serving effectively as a way of creating a timed window into which the children would go to sleep. This focus on bedtime routines also therefore showed us how often for participants, getting off to sleep was prioritized in this routine, above saving energy. This is interesting to note in that there is likewise a future-oriented element to this, in that we might interpret the need to get to sleep as part of the process of preparing for the following day.

Timers were also used within other elements of everyday routines. For instance, one teenager in the LEEDR study used the same song on his mobile phone every morning to time his shower. It was a favourite song, which he knew lasted around three minutes, thus helping him to 'check the time' his shower took. He then kept the music running while drying his hair and getting dressed in his room, before going downstairs and switching to the family's tablet to watch YouTube videos over breakfast. Interestingly, this

FIGURE 2.4 *Participants on the LEEDR project used a range of timing technologies and techniques for varying purposes. A toothbrush timer was used to extend brushing time; a radio was left on in the background to make the home feel less quiet and to indicate timing through participants' tacit knowledge of broadcasting schedules; TVs, radios and stereo systems were left on at bedtime to turn themselves off via timers or at the end of a CD; ovens were left on timers for food preparation to end in time for the family to return home (slow cookers fulfilled a similar function); and washing machines, dishwashers and lamps were left on timers to come on at specified times during the evening or night, and in the case of lighting in order to create the right atmosphere as well as for security purposes. © LEEDR.*

personalization of his showering routine also informed his conception of possible future shower systems, which he saw as coming with integrated timers and personal customization (including favourite songs), showing again how people's personal visions of futures build on their existing realms of experience. Some participants also used digital displays linked to their toothbrushes to time their brushing – in this case to extend the time they would spend on brushing. People also used egg timers for this and for showering purposes. In general, we have interpreted this to understand that participants were especially conscious of time when it came to bathroom uses because there was a sense of competing for the same space as well as a sensitivity towards the use of resources.

The use of timers in family homes is not a new phenomenon; however, as we have shown in this section, digital technologies invite particular ways of timing TV and radio time as well as of other everyday activities. Timing is moreover a culturally relevant way of engaging with temporality at home, and it enables people to structure certain elements of their day. Timing in the cases discussed was always connected to the accomplishment of certain priorities. In these particular examples it involved limiting certain types of resource use or activity – such as energy use or sleeping. Yet, as these different examples show, while using a timer to reduce the amount of time a person spends showering or so that the washing machine would come on at night might reduce energy use or shift it from peak energy demand times, it could also use energy in ways that could be interpreted as unnecessary – since technologies that were left on in standby mode when switched off by a timer would still consume energy during the night.

We propose therefore that attention to timing offers one way to understand and account for the temporalities of home, everyday intentionalities and the priorities that guide everyday activities in homes. Where it is found to be culturally and socially embedded activity, it might also be considered as a site for possibly meaningful interventions for change, which could be developed collaboratively with participants.

Modes of anticipation in the home

One of the numerous ways in which people live *with* the future, or orientate themselves towards the future in everyday life, is through anticipation. While anticipation does not exclusively emerge in the home, it can be part of one's work practices and experiences, or it can be related to everyday situations of waiting, such as in commuting (Ehn and Lofgren 2010); some forms of anticipation can be regarded as specific to domestic environments, as we will show below.

In her work, Roxana Moroşanu gained a set of interesting insights on anticipation in the home, by designing and using a self-interviewing with video method: the Five Cups of Tea technique. We outline the Five Cups of Tea method in more detail in Chapter 5; briefly however, this method asked the participants to self-interview themselves in solitude while preparing and having a cup of tea and responding to a few sets of questions. For every cup of tea they filmed, the people who took part in the research were asked to mention what they did before the 'break for a cuppa' and what they were planning to do afterwards. In talking about their next activity, people often tried to break it down into tasks or segments, and they described the tasks and placed them in a temporal order, as a way of preparing themselves and of anticipating the way in which they will do that specific activity.

For one participant, Emma, the cup of tea break provided the opportunity to sit down after an hour or so of multitasking around the house, tidying and cleaning in the aftermath of the school run, and to prepare for the next activity that she saw as something more difficult and that necessitated more concentration on her part. This was keeping the accounts for an after-school group that she helped run. While having her cup of tea, Emma said that she was going to sit at the living room table in front of her laptop in order to do this accounting job, and that she would look for a set of older receipts that she would need to log in a spreadsheet, in order to bring the account up to date. Thinking about and describing the activity to the video camera was for Emma a way to make herself ready to start that job. By anticipating the series of tasks that she was going to perform, Emma was rehearsing the activity, and she could also imagine it being finished. The ways in which people anticipated the temporal horizon that would follow the completion of a task, as well as the anticipation of the task itself, were addressed in the materials that resulted from the use of the Five Cups of Tea method.

The forms of anticipation enacted by people who participated with Roxana in this activity can be regarded as short-term anticipation because they refer to a set of actions that are planned, or expected, to occur soon. This is also the case of the series of tasks that make up other domestic activities, such as cooking. For example, the action that starts the process of cooking is often anticipatory: boiling the kettle before peeling and chopping vegetables, or switching the oven on so that it would reach the desired temperature before the cake composition is actually ready can be regarded as short-term anticipatory actions related to the embodied knowledge of performing a task. Instead, long-term anticipation, or looking forward to, relies more on imagination. Looking forward to an event, such as a holiday, changes the way in which people do things in the present in subtler ways that might be related to how the present is emotionally perceived more than to practical actions.

Other forms of anticipation in domestic settings can be regarded in relation to practices of care-giving; to one's knowledge of how someone – or something – is likely to act; and to knowing about the routines of the other family members and being able to imagine what they are doing – at what point they are in their day – at any moment. These examples, as well as the issue concerning the possible impacts that actions related to anticipation can have on domestic energy demand, are discussed in more detail elsewhere (Moroşanu 2016a). While here they were discussed as ways of living with the future, modes of anticipation in domestic settings can also be regarded in relation to practices of making multitemporality with one's home (Moroşanu 2016b).

As these examples and Moroşanu's wider work show, anticipatory modes are therefore important elements of the way everyday life in the home is organized and experienced. This raises interesting questions for design in homes, in that it introduces a way of thinking about what people do as having an ongoing focus on what might (but will not necessarily always) come next, and that this can have an affective dimension, as noted above in relation to the idea of anticipation as caring. This, we argue, merits further investigation in design ethnography research, in relation to how, for instance, the affective qualities of anticipation might be harnessed for beneficial forms of collaborative change-making.

Imagining future homes as part of other configurations of hope

Future homes are not things that people imagine in ways that are separate from other aspects of their lives, but that imagining is always situated, whether in moments of anticipation (as in the examples from Moroşanu's research outlined in the previous section) or in projects of home, as in the examples from Pink's (2004) earlier research, also discussed above. This point was also demonstrated in *Laundry Lives*, where towards the end of the documentary participants were asked to reflect on their futures from two perspectives. First they speak about their hopes for their future domestic technologies, as discussed above (see Figures 2.1 and 2.2). However, when asked to reflect on what they wanted for the future, their responses showed that actually these hopes and aspirations for new technologies were subsumed, for all of the participants with not yet adult children, within what appeared to be a culturally specific affective hope for the future – that is, a vision of a better future for their children. As Pink argues in the documentary, if we want to design for homes in ways that will be coherent with people's dreams and hopes for the future, we need to attend to these kinds of hopes (and those of other people in other contexts) as inseparable from the ways that people will live in their homes, with other people and with technological possibilities (Pink and Astari 2015).

Design ethnography temporalities

Above we have outlined a series of ways in which temporalities of ethnography and of home are perceived, constituted and structured. We have discussed how traditionally ethnography has a past orientation. Yet, as we have shown in the previous section of this chapter, once an ethnographic approach is opened up to considering the future, new possibilities for investigation arise. Acknowledging the future in this way has enabled us to explore where it is situated in the present, and how its perception forms part of the way everyday life is organized and experienced. Some of the research findings discussed above might be culturally specific to, or at least culturally inflected by, the English context, which forms the main source of our examples. Nevertheless, we have shown, future temporalities also appear as part of everyday life in the home in similar, if not in exactly the same, ways in Spain and Indonesia.

While it is impossible to know or predict what will happen next in any certain way, in contrast the temporalities of home are often predictable in their organization, since they are followed or reconstituted each day in similar (but never absolutely identical) ways, and often across different households. Some of them overlap or crisscross each other, or follow on. Together they tell us that everyday life in the home can be interpreted as an ongoing set of activities, many of which can be seen to be orientated towards what is going to happen next or what might happen at a more distant moment. This is not surprising if we consider that life ongoingly involves fantasizing about, or imagining, what to do next, across a range of different timescales, all of which might need to be considered simultaneously and relationally. It is important to note that imagining futures is not the same as planning futures that will actually play out. Nevertheless, as existing research has shown (e.g. Irving 2017), when understanding futures we need to account for the reality that as yet unknown or unexpected contingencies that emerge from the present will intervene in what happens next, sometimes in ways that go unnoticed, but that can often be uncovered through ethnography.

Understanding people's everyday temporalities of home thus offers a novel way of considering the relationship between everyday life and design: design, as we have noted in the previous chapter is a future-oriented discipline but cannot be predictive. The challenge therefore is to ask how to unite the future focus of design, the anticipatory modes of everyday life, and a future-oriented ethnographic practice, to make interventions that will be captured by people's existing engagements with the temporalities of their worlds. Before approaching this question, we prefigure that discussion with a summary of the broader context in which the different temporalities of ethnography and design have been pitched in relation to each other.

Jamer Hunt (2010) has suggested that temporality and intervention are two key differences between design and anthropology/ethnography. For Hunt the temporalities of anthropology, focused on detailing the present (soon to become the past), are distinguished from those of design, which is focused on the future. He brings them together through a discussion of critical design projects, which, he suggests, 'compel us to reconsider how the present is futuring – to use [the designer] Tony Fry's words – and how we may still have a chance to reconfigure that future potentiality'. He suggests that critical design can 'slow down the future and its defuturing by prefiguring us in those future moments. They bring together the analytical incisiveness of an ethnographer's eye with the materializing vision of a designer' (2010: 44). While Hunt's efforts to show how ethnographic principles might be engaged in design research seek to resolve differences between the disciplines, they do not reconcile the differences between a discipline that focuses on the past, and another that focuses on the future or between a discipline that problematizes the idea of intervention and one that intervenes as a matter of course. More recent discussions of these issues have not resolved these tensions either, but they have shown the benefit of acknowledging them as creative tensions. As Ton Otto and Rachel Charlotte Smith put it,

> Design is clearly *future oriented*; its success is measured by the relevance the designed products and conceptual solutions have for people's everyday lives. Although anthropology has an interest in social change and people's imaginations of the future, as a discipline it lacks tools and practices to actively engage and collaborate in people's formation of their futures. One of design anthropology's challenges is to develop such tools and practices of collaborative future making. (2013: 3)

We take up this challenge with reference to design and the home in this book. We argue that a future-focused ethnographic practice, which engages with developing new understandings of how futures are part of the everyday present of life as lived out in homes, is at least complementary to the aspirations of design, and should at best be seen as a point where ethnography and design become part of the same practice.

Summing up

In this chapter we have argued that a design ethnography for the home needs to be based on a reconceptualized relationship between everyday life in the home, ethnography and design, and that this entails aligning the temporalities of these processes. In doing so, we need to attend to the idea that the future is made in the present, and is not a separate or distant place that we will inhabit in an unknown time (Pink and Salazar 2017); the opportunity to do ethnographies of the possible, probable or of potentialities (Halse 2013); the anticipatory logics and forms of future-thinking that are part of some contemporary societies, and how these impact on our practice as researchers and designers (e.g. Kinsley 2012; Anderson 2009) and; how the anticipatory modes of everyday life (Moroşanu 2016) are relevant to ethnographic and design practice.

As we show in the next chapter, this approach is particularly applicable for thinking through how we might engage critically as ethnographers and designers with future utopian visions of our home environments, such as that of the smart home, and how we might think in alternative ways about the home as an environment.

3

Environments

Introduction

In this chapter we conceptualize the home as a continually changing environment, and consider how ethnography and design can create beneficial ways of understanding and participating in this process of change. Building on the insights generated in the last chapter, we have already begun to outline an understanding of the home as a temporal context for ethnographies and for design. Here we build on that idea and pursue our argument further through an emphasis on the processuality of home environments. This perspective is informative because it allows us to consider how home is ongoingly reconstituted, and what things, processes and activities this might entail. It advances our consideration of the temporality of home in a new direction because it shows how the human-focused temporalities and perceptions of time and future that we discussed in the last chapter are also part of a world where non-human constituents are likewise implicated in processes of change, in determining what might happen next, and might too be involved in trajectories that can be thought of as having an orientation towards the future, if not an future-focused intentionality or imagination. Accounting for environments as constituted through the entanglement of diverse processes, things and activities that are ongoingly changing is increasingly popular in the social sciences and humanities. The approach to this developed here, is influenced by the work of Ingold, whereby 'the environment, is in the first place, a world we live in, and not a world we look at. We *inhabit* our environment: we are part of it; and through this practice of habitation it becomes part of us too' (2010: 96). We perceive, experience and know our environment as we move through it (2010: 45). Such environments are in ongoing processes of change, not only in relation to human and living elements, but also through material and technological elements, as is shown through the growing emphasis in literatures across human geography and material culture studies on how things are always in processes of decay, damage or repair (e.g. Deslivey 2006; Domínguez Rubio 2016). Seeing environments of home as being constituted as such, we argue, has significance for how we both understand, and seek to make interventions towards change in, everyday life in the home. Yet neither this configuration of home nor its potential are usually accounted for in either applied academic ethnography or solutions-based design research and practice focused on homes.

In developing this discussion we select three key elements of the contemporary home that we propose deserve particular attention due to their relevance to academic scholarship, design and society. We consider the home in terms of its qualities and affordances as a *material*, *digital* and sensory and affective *atmospheric* environment, which human activity is both a part of and constitutive of. Each of these categories of thing is always in progress, although the things change, decay and become repaired or renewed at different velocities and in different ways. We will argue that without this perspective on home the search for intervention opportunities runs the risk of missing the complex relations between human activities and the situated contexts that frame and are constituted by them.

As noted in Chapter 1, the idea of considering the digital elements of the environment of home implies the notion of the smart home. However, rather than taking or assuming the smart home as a starting point and as a future reality, we propose beginning with the theoretical–methodological question of home as a configuration of things and processes that include the digital. This is moreover important to consider because in the near digital future it is likely that the smart home will not be a universal phenomenon that is equally distributed globally, or uniformly constituted, experienced or engaged with. Moreover, just as with the concept of 'off-grid' living – (away from energy infrastructures), we imagine that some people will opt for non-smart home living. Therefore, as noted in Chapter 1, instead of starting with the premise of the smart home, we propose taking the notion of the digital materiality of homes and the way this is experienced sensorially and affectively as a starting point. This invites us to consider how the digital and material are always implicated in homes, even if both categories or the relationships between them are not manifested in obvious or explicit ways. Digital materiality has previously been discussed across a range of disciplines that are also concerned with homes, including digital anthropology, architecture, design and media studies (Horst and Miller 2012; Willman et al. 2013; Gramazio and Kohler 2008; van Dijck 2004), thus representing an interdisciplinary concern for considering the relationality between the digital and material. Here we use Pink, Ardevol and Lanzeni's (2016: 10–11) processual conceptualization, for which the relationality of the digital material does not begin 'with an a priori definition about what is digital and what is material'. It instead suggests that we understand 'digital materiality as a process, and as emergent, not as an end product or finished object'. In this reasoning, digital materiality is what can be referred to as a 'thing' rather than an 'object'. This relies on a definition where 'things are alive because they leak' (Ingold 2008: 10); things are not closed or discrete or complete whereas objects are conceptualized as being such (Pink, Ardevol and Lanzeni 2016: 10–11). Therefore digital materiality is emergent from the configurations of the environment of home. Here we are interested in how the home can be the site for its making, its experience and intervention in relation to it.

In what follows, we first explore what can be achieved by approaching the home through its materiality, and examine how material culture studies of home have become implicated with design anthropology approaches. We then focus on the implications of shifting the focus from materiality to a digital materiality, which could also be understood as part of the atmosphere of home. However, we stress that although the structure of this chapter runs through from materiality, the digital to the sensory and atmospheric home, analytically these three categories of everyday life in the contemporary home are rarely separable. Therefore, we treat each of these three as possible entry points into what we discuss below as being a digital–material–sensory environment of home.

The materiality of home

The materiality of home has long since been an emphasis in anthropological studies of home, established as such by the early work of Danny Miller (1988). Approaching the home through its material culture has therefore been shown to be a useful way into understanding the complex entanglements of relationships that homes and people who live in them are implicated in. It has also been a particularly fruitful route through which to consider their consumption (see Bucchli 2013: 118). For example, Miller's seminal work in this field demonstrated how the ways in which participants in his research decorated the kitchens of their council flats in the United Kingdom could be seen to be representative of their situatedness in a set of economic and power relations with the state. The trajectory of this work has impacted on a range of studies which offer key perspectives on the roles played by material culture in everyday life in the home and show how and why 'things' matter (e.g. Miller 2001, 2008). Significantly, also inspired by Miller's work in this area, consumption was understood in relation to how people appropriated objects (Miller 1988, 2001), themes that, as discussed below, were also reflected in media studies undertaken in homes. As Bucchli's (2013) impressive review of research undertaken over the last forty or so years, into the material culture of the domestic interior across a range of different cultures, shows there is a strong body of academic scholarship that supports the idea that people are ongoingly participating in what he, drawing on Pauline Garvey's work (which itself draws on Giddens ideas), refers to as 'continuous revision' (Garvey 2001; Bucchli 2013: 135). Bucchli folds this back into discussions of the constitution of selfhood, through consumption, which has been a key theme in the material culture approaches to the home (2013: 135). Thus this body of work offers insight into thinking about how the materiality of home is inextricably bound up with lives, identities, gender relations and much more. It also indicates that people are ongoingly *doing* things with material culture – what has previously been called appropriation.

If we now switch theoretical registers to return to the idea of everyday improvisation that we outlined in Chapter 1, we can go beyond considering how the material culture of home is appropriated and/or used as part of how people understand and constitute who they are. In addition to this we can ask how it is part of the ways that people improvise in everyday life and also how consumption can be thought of as involving improvisation. The material culture of home, be it consumer products or firewood, becomes tangled up with the ways that people navigate the contingencies of everyday life and the small solutions they improvise to deal with everyday challenges. By seeing everyday ways of engaging with the materiality of the home as a form of improvisation, we advance this discussion further to explore how the materiality of home can be understood as a starting point for applied and design research and intervention in the home, rather than as an end point for interventions, or as a conclusion for academic scholarship around the home. Moreover by acknowledging that material, sensory and digital elements of home are also involved in processes of decay, damage, repair or renewal, it becomes clear that the environment of home is a moving ecology of things and processes. We argue that a focus on the home through elements of its materiality (situated in this way) can bring novel insights that go beyond the scope of existing design research about homes and extend further the ways that anthropological ethnography can be engaged for impact in the world. The intention behind this approach in our own work has been to use a materiality prism to lead to critical understandings about how and why activities that are problematic for environmental sustainability are lived out as part of everyday life, even when people are aware of their problematic nature. We have also used the findings of such work to propose how particular design 'solutions' cannot directly address such problems. We next outline two examples of how materiality, contingency and improvisation come together in the home.

Whereas much of the past research in the field of material culture studies of the home focused on the production of self-identity (e.g. Miller 1988, 2001), the two examples we discuss here relate to elements of the mundane materiality of home in relation to everyday contingencies. First, we build our existing work to refigure laundry as part of the materiality of home (Pink 2012; Pink et al. 2015). We show how in the British context where indoor drying is a common practice, this can be framed as a 'problem', which wastes energy and creates issues of environmental health, yet has no simple solution. In Yogyakarta in Indonesia in contrast, where laundry is often (but as shown in the following example, not always) dried outside, its materiality is part of everyday worlds in different ways. Within the LEEDR project our interest in laundry was driven by its status as a mundane but inescapable background activity in the home, as well as an interest in understanding how the energy consumption of the home was impacted by the use of washing machines and tumble dryers along with the use of other technologies for indoor drying in the United Kingdom, including radiators. In the UK context indoor drying of laundry using radiator or other heating technologies is considered problematic not only from the energy demand perspective but also due to its environmental health implications, as it leads to increased humidity (Porteous et al. 2014).

However, as our ethnographic research in homes revealed, because indoor drying is part of how people live in their homes in the United Kingdom, this makes it difficult to bring about change to alleviate the issues it raises around health and energy. Viewing these questions through the prism of the materiality of home offers us a way to conceptualize this situation. Elsewhere we have discussed in depth how indoor drying is embedded in homes. The following extract from our work in this area describes through the example of one participant's home a quite typical scenario of how ongoing laundry processes, while often thought of as happening in the background, and being invisible, are in fact continually present in the home and form part of its materiality and sensoriality:

Roxana arrived at Denise's home ... .On this Tuesday visit there was laundry drying on racks in the kitchen – three clotheshorses – two from Sunday, tea towels from Monday. It was May and Denise explained how at this time of the year some things seemed to take longer to dry while other, possibly smaller items, didn't take so long, and others might be out in front of a radiator which meant they would get dry. She pointed out that drying, and from our point of view the way that laundry becomes part of the materiality and texture of home, depends on the time of the year, telling Roxana that: 'If it was winter, I'd probably be moving these around a lot more, putting them on the radiators, rotating them, just when I was around.' In contrast in summer they might dry overnight. As the encounter continued we learned more about how laundry becomes part of the sensory aesthetic of home. Denise described how where the laundry is positioned in the room also matters for drying, that it ideally would not be done in the kitchen, and on a nice day it would be outside. Other contingencies, materialities and arrangements of home also impacted on where and how laundry would be situated. Another option would be 'if my little box room wasn't full of rubbish I'd probably have them in there, cos I don't really want them picking up cooking smells'; she also did not particularly want guests to see the washing as it dried in the home. It was not only the drying laundry, however, that formed part of the visible texture of home. Clean sheets lay on the armchair in the master bedroom from when they were washed one and a half weeks ago (Pink, Leder Mackley and Moroşanu 2013).

As this and other examples from our research (and Pink's earlier work, e.g. Pink 2012) demonstrate, the ways that participants dried laundry in their homes were bound up with a series of everyday contingencies. We also learned how participants used their own in-depth and experience-based knowledge about where to best dry items in the home, for example, where sunlight came in through the window, which radiators worked best, and where under floor heating trails went through the home. Thus, they engaged their unspoken sensory ways of knowing and improvising in the environment of home, and their appreciation for the flows of warmth that move through it at different times of the day and different seasons, in order to be able to accomplish the task of drying laundry adequately. While on the one hand, it is relevant to acknowledge that indoor drying is environmentally problematic in some climates, on the other, as our research shows, indoor drying is simultaneously part of people's complex relationships with and ways of knowing in their everyday home environments.

We now focus in more closely on the relationship between material culture and the improvisatory nature of human activity in the home, which was highlighted in Chapter 1. In this example, drawing a contrast to the digital technologies discussed below, we focus on how low-tech improvisation (or what in other contexts is referred to as innovation or appropriation) with simple technologies can create key environmental sustainability interventions. Everyday improvisation could involve improvising processes and creating new routines, as well as improvising with material objects. Often the two were part of the same activity, which also engaged technologies, interpreted in a broader sense. The examples presented in Figures 3.1 and 3.2 make two key points. First, these material-technological solutions are emergent outcomes of our everyday life negotiations with the persons, things and processes that constitute home. Second, they need to be accounted for when considering the relationship between everyday and designed solutions. Both of these examples focus on how participants in different research projects used sticks to improvise low-tech solutions to everyday challenges that made their lives more convenient, reduced energy costs, and also responded to environmental sustainability challenges. In both cases it is also clear that the particular solutions developed

FIGURE 3.1 *In England, Alan took the stick that he kept hidden behind the TV and explained how to solve the problem of all these cables and plugs being hard to reach to switch off behind the TV: 'All I do is just reach down ... and just run all of the switches off.' Still image from Video 6, at www.energyanddigitalliving.com* © *LEEDR.*

FIGURE 3.2 *In the* Laundry Lives *documentary, Adi explained how in his everyday life in Indonesia he used a stick to hang his laundry high up underneath the transparent roof of the area of the house where the washing machine was located so that his family's clothes would dry effectively in the house.* © *Sarah Pink and Nadia Astari 2015.*

FIGURE 3.3 *Ning and Mbok Jinah talking about the washing machine and not damaging clothes. © Sarah Pink and Nadia Astari 2015.*

by participants responded to the particular challenges of, in one case switching off the electricity at night so it would not be on standby mode, and in the other, of finding an effective way of drying laundry at home, which was particularly suited to the material layout of the home. In one case the back of the TV being difficult to access without a stick, and in the other case the high transparent ceiling of the room laundry being dried in, being effective for drying laundry, but difficult to reach. Both examples explicitly also draw on the participants' everyday knowledge about their homes and the people they live with in them.

Finally, the materiality of home (as is also the case for the digital and atmospheric elements of home) is always in progress itself. Material decay, repair and renewal are all part of home, and engagement with them is a part of everyday life in the home. In Chapter 2, we have described how the home changed materially and conceptually as a project where humans intentionally played a role in reshaping the home over time and through routine activities. However the material elements of home also decay, or become damaged, and this forms part of their relationships to humans and other technologies or elements of home. Two examples show this well. First, in *Laundry Lives*, participants mention how they will not put certain of their clothes in the washing machine due to their concerns that they will be damaged. In the case of one household this was taken very seriously, and the participants in question, Ning and her helper, Mbok Jinah, emphasized that they only used the washing machine on the spin cycle. They washed all the clothes by hand first, because they believed that the clothes would deteriorate more quickly if washed in the machine.

Another example of how the home contains elements of material change that are not immediately obvious to researchers came to the surface when Sarah and Kerstin were visiting and video recording with Alan, one of the LEEDR participants (see also www.energanddigitalliving.com, where elements of this

FIGURE 3.4 *Alan showed us the walls.* © *LEEDR.*

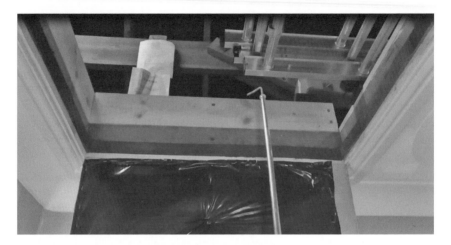

FIGURE 3.5 *Alan showed us the loft.* © *LEEDR.*

example are discussed). When we left Alan's house we realized that as he had shown it to us he had revealed a whole dimension of its materiality that would otherwise have been invisible to us. As we walked through the bedrooms to the home he explained to us how he had insulated the walls and then papered them in the way chosen by his family. As we observed the walls, all we could see were carefully decorated rooms, but as he explained the work that had gone before, we realized that he could feel a very different materiality and that his understandings of the sensory affordances of the walls would be different to ours. Our understanding of this became clearer as he opened the loft hatch and invited us to step up, to see how he had insulated this area of the home. We began to understand better how the house seemed to him, and as he showed us, how we might interpret the visual differences between the different rooftops in his neighbourhood in relation to the amount of frozen snow they hosted, and what this indicated to him about the quality of his own insulation project.

The atmospheres of home

The material culture studies focus on the home has, as we have seen in the last section, had an enduring impact on the ways in which the home has been studied ethnographically. However as the examples discussed there show, the material culture of homes is experienced in ways that go beyond the analysis of the earlier material culture studies of home – through the senses, the emotions and other intangible and sometimes invisible elements of everyday life in the home that surpass the earlier emphasis on the visible and material. As we have also argued, the materiality of the home might be better thought of as a form of digital materiality, which will be evident and present to different degrees and in different ways in different homes. Building on these insights, we now explore two key theoretical and practical moves that have impacted on how we understand these invisible environments of home. First, what has been called the 'sensory turn' (Howes 2005) in scholarship has drawn our attention to the ways in which human sensory perception is implicated in the making and experiencing of home. This has meant that studies of the home have also moved on beyond materiality to account for the immaterial or intangible textures, odours or sounds of home (e.g. Tacchi 1998; Pink 2004, 2012). This invisible and intangible layer of everyday environments forms a key element of the ways that the environment of home is experienced and made, and, we argue, this is something that we cannot ignore in either ethnographic or design practice. This is because these tacit, unspoken and sometimes unseen ways of experiencing the home are also integral to the things people *do* in their homes. They might indeed be the very aspects of life in the home that design interventions can effectively respond to.

Second, there has recently been a surge in interest in theories of atmosphere (e.g. Böhme 1993, 2013), across human geography (Anderson 2009; Bissell 2011; Edensor 2012, 2014) and particularly in anthropology with reference to homes (e.g. Shaw 2014; Bille et al. 2014). This work has drawn our attention to the ways that home feels, beyond sensory perception towards a greater recognition of the unspoken sensory, emotional, mundane and intense feelings that are generated through our embodied relationships with the material and intangible environments of home. As we have argued elsewhere, drawing on Ingold's (2010) work on atmosphere and environment, 'we can understand the atmospheres as emergent from processes of making. That is from the encounters between people, materials and other elements of the environments of which they are part (e.g. air, light, warmth, scents).' This conceptualization also emphasizes the themes developed in the last section since 'atmospheres are not as such products but they are produced or emergent ongoingly as people improvise their ways through the world' (Pink and Leder Mackley 2016). While there has often been something of an emphasis on atmospheres as being 'intensive' (Anderson 2009: 80), or as producing intensities (Bille et al. 2014) in existing work, we have argued elsewhere for a closer consideration of 'atmosphere as mundane and as always present' (Pink, Leder Mackley and Moroşanu 2015b). As discussed in Chapter 4, this conceptualization of atmosphere is also connected with movement through the home, and is part of a way of theorizing home as processual. We therefore argue that atmospheres are not simply things that sometimes emerge. Rather they should be understood as being already there, and always changing. The merit of focusing on atmosphere as an ethnographic and analytical concept is that by bringing it to the foreground of the analysis we can investigate how specific elements of home – such as light, heating or sound – are used or improvised with. As we have argued:

> If atmospheres are conceptualized as already part of the world that we inhabit, therefore ... the core question is not *if* there is an atmosphere. Instead it centres on how we might: identify empirically the contingencies that constitute particular atmospheres; understand their qualities and affordances; and, use this knowledge to generate insights into mundane everyday life worlds where atmospheres, people, things and processes together constitute everyday environments. (Pink, Leder Mackley and Moroşanu 2015b)

Moreover, atmospheres, although they are not usually theorized as such, tend to also involve technologies as well as material qualities of home; therefore, a focus on them can help us to understand how technologies are inseparable from the ways that we experience the environments of home.

At the core of our ethnographic research in homes has been the concept of 'feeling right'. The way in which this concept can be engaged in ethnographic and design practice is discussed further in Chapter 5. Here it informs how we understand the ways in which atmospheres of home are something that is 'felt'. The ongoing processes through which the atmospheres of home are constituted involve both human intentionality (discussed further in the next chapter) and non-human processes, including those of materials and intangible elements. Pink's earlier research showed how different sounds and smells formed part of the making of what she termed the 'sensory home' and that these were often implicated in processes of everyday activity (Pink 2004, 2012). In some cases this referred to the spatiality of home; for instance, Pink describes how this plays out in England:

> For Andrew, a university lecturer who lived alone, listening to Radio 4 was part of his experience of being in the kitchen, and part of his sensory experience of activities he engaged in in his kitchen, whether he was cooking a meal, cleaning or just coming down from his study to make a cup of tea. As such it formed part of a sensory space he moved in and out of. (2004: 71)

In other cases, the sensory home was explicitly constituted and/or reconstituted (even if slightly differently each time) through processes of renewal, including cleaning and refreshing the home, for instance through opening windows. For instance, in Spain, Rafaela spoke about how

> for her dirt was not just a visual experience but also olfactory, as she described: 'I can smell cleanliness, its inevitable. I go into a house and I see dust and I smell the dust and I say: "There's a lot of dust in here." I can't help it. I can't stand dust. I have to get rid of it. That's why I use the vacuum cleaner, because I can't stand dust.' (Pink 2004: 68)

In this section we explore the notion of atmospheres of home through a focus on how people use lighting and darkness to generate certain feelings of home.

FIGURE 3.6 *Lighting the English living room.* © *LEEDR.*

Lighting and the use of lighting technologies offer an ideal example through which to examine how non-tangible but 'felt' elements of home participate in the constitution of atmospheres, because lighting has been researched ethnographically across different cultural contexts, thus offering insights into the making of diverse and culturally specific ways of feeling or atmospheres.

Lighting is moreover interesting in relation to its energy consumption. Lighting makes up only about 3 per cent of the energy consumption in the home (Palmer and Cooper 2013), which for some would make it a less pressing concern. Yet, in the United Kingdom, 'Most homes now have more light fittings than they did in 1970 – especially in kitchens and bathrooms. Lighting in kitchens, in particular, tends to be a much higher specification than it was in the past. Many homes have replaced a single fluorescent strip light with many high output spotlights' (Palmer and Cooper 2013: 37). Moreover, if we focus solely on electricity, lighting in fact accounts for around 18 per cent of typical household's electricity bill, which means that significant savings could still be made through reducing its use (Energy Saving Trust n.d.). Yet while people might be aware of these issues (or in some cases contest them), even when they are keen to save energy, other priorities can dominate. Atmosphere offers a good route through which to analyse how such priorities play out. For example Mikkel Bille's research into the relationship between lighting in homes in Denmark, the concept of *hygge* or 'cosiness' and energy saving showed how the atmospheres that emerge from conventional configurations of lighting are a priority, which makes it difficult for energy saving lighting to be accepted. He comments that

> the relationship between atmospheres and new technologies, is that understanding the appreciation of specific material qualities of light, the

ecstasies of the bulb's colour reproduction and temperature, the patina and multi-sensuality of orchestrating lightscapes through the shadows, the flickering flames, and the glow from the subdued lighting, is at the heart of understanding the contestation against adopting a new technology. (Bille 2015b)

Second, lighting (including the use of electric lights, daylight, mobile phone lights, and possibly other sources) tends to be an activity, an everyday task, done ongoingly, throughout the day, as people continually adapt to changes in the environments they inhabit, as they move through them. Indeed lighting, digital media use (discussed below) and a range of other activities, things and processes, such as heating, opening windows and more (some of which are discussed in the next chapter in more detail), are equally ongoing and part of how atmospheres of home are constituted. As Pink and Leder Mackley have argued, drawing on Ingold's work on atmosphere and environment, 'We can understand the atmospheres as emergent from processes of making. That is from the encounters between people, materials and other elements of the environments of which they are part (e.g. air, light, warmth, scents). Atmospheres are not as such products but they are produced or emergent ongoingly as people improvise their ways through the world' (Pink and Leder Mackely 2016). Therefore our focus on lighting here is not because we believe that it is lighting above other activities that makes atmospheres of home, or that it is theoretically a practice or something that should be turned into an independent analytical unit. Instead, the study of things and processes like lighting enables us entry points into the environments of homes. Therefore our interest in lighting is way to investigate

how we might: identify empirically the contingencies that constitute particular atmospheres; understand their qualities and affordances; and, use this knowledge to generate insights into mundane everyday life worlds where atmospheres, people, things and processes together constitute everyday environments. (Pink, Leder Mackley and Moroşanu 2015b)

Lighting is not a discrete practice, but it is relational to and interwoven with other constituents and processes of home. At bedtime in our research, this included other humans, cats, dogs, locks, doors, televisions, sounds and books. Opening the curtains in the morning is likewise part of the process of making the morning home, as well as being a means of lighting rooms. Curtains (and blinds) are also a technology of lighting, yet they are not only used to keep light out or let it in, but also to enable to curtail other flows, of air, warmth, heat and more. Domestic lighting can also include the opportunistic use of automated street lighting to illuminate some areas of the home where it is allowed to seep through what we have elsewhere written of as the porous boundaries of home. It can also involve light flows from mobile phones and other devices carried through the home (see for example videos 32 and 33 at www.energyanddigitalliving.com). Here lighting is therefore part of and relative to a set of contingencies of home, and just as laundry discussed above offers a material culture-focused entry point into the environment of home, lighting offers a sensorial entry point. However both lighting and laundry equally form part of what we might see as the texture of home. Indeed the LEEDR study revealed that people had diverse and contingent ways of using lighting in the making of atmospheres of home. For some participants a room only felt right when all of the available lights were switched on or the space was generally well lit. This was partly related to wanting to be able to see. Partly participants described needing the light to also lighten their mood, thus bringing to the fore the affective dimension of atmospheres, whereas others preferred what is perhaps more commonly described as 'atmospheric' lighting, that is, the selected use of individual lamps that would light specific corners of a room. Especially families with young children demonstrated to us how they would use lighting strategically at night, borrowing light from adjoining rooms or keeping lights on a dimmer during the night and in the early morning when wanting to 'ease' into the day, thus using light to help produce a particular sensory environment or atmosphere for the benefit of their children. Others described using lighting as a signal, either to outsiders – for example, keeping lighting on timers so as to deter possible intruders – or as a welcoming device for family members who are out at night, whereby lighting becomes a form of caring.

An example of how the trails of contingencies that determined how and when people use lighting was demonstrated well by Rhodes, a participant in the LEEDR project. The wider context of our research with Rhodes is discussed in a methodological article (Pink and Leder Mackley 2012) where we explain how she had developed a sequence of bedtime activities which involved her using both the ceiling spotlights and the bedside lamp in her bedroom, since she needed to put on the stronger lights while the low energy consuming bedside lamp warmed up, and was ready to participate in her ultimate project of creating the right atmosphere for her bedtime room, which also included the TV being on (see Pink and Leder Mackley 2012, Clip 3, or https://www.youtube.com/watch?v=vEwBRwjPBzl). While Rhodes was committed to low energy use, as the example shows, she needed to play out this commitment in relation to a series of other everyday life priorities, which had impeded her economical use of lighting at bedtime. She is a good example of how, as we have noted in Chapter 1, being aware that one is not saving energy through everyday actions is not necessarily enough to make it possible to change the everyday processes of objects that are implicated in this. Indeed, as this and other examples show, lighting is not an element of home that can exist independently of other elements. The example cited above showed how lighting the bedroom is part of a series of contingencies of home. Rhodes also explained how lighting was part of the process of making home over time, where things are moved around, and might be used, disused and appropriated for new uses.

Our research has also shown how lighting and digital media routines can become interwoven with each other in the making of atmospheres of home. In the previous chapter we discussed bedtime routines as transition moments, and elements of the temporality of the home. These routines specifically combined ways of using lighting and ways of using digital technologies and media throughout the routine. Lee (see video 32 at www.energyanddigitalliving. com) put his living room light on so he would remember to go back into the room to switch off the TV, he used his smartphone as a light, and his switching off routine involved switching off both lights and digital media. In the next section we extend the discussion further, to reflect on how digital technologies are implicated in the materiality and atmospheres of home.

Finally, we note that the examples in this section focused on how lighting participates in the constitution of atmospheres of home. Similar analyses could be under taken that draw on the work of scholars who have investigated, for instance, the sounds of home (Duffy and Waitt 2013) or the materiality of air in homes (Hauge 2013) or who have put other categories of sensory experience at the centre of their investigations of home.

The digital–material–atmospheric home

Most recently the notion of the home as an environment in which the digital and material are part of the same locality, and as a context that stretches beyond locality, has become increasingly prominent. While, as noted in Chapter 1, these shifts are often discussed under the guise of the possible future smart home, our argument is that before we can even begin to think about the possible ways in which smart homes should be designed, we need a viable theoretical framework through which to understand how people may live with possible future technologies; an ethnographic methodology through which to comprehend how people and technologies become part of the same environments of home; and a base of existing ethnographic understandings through which to begin to develop sets of principles for understanding the forms of difference, kinds of feelings, ways of being, improvisations, types of resistance and other implications that emerge when people begin to live with technologies in ways that are at once new and continuous with their existing habits. Such understandings are moreover likely to be culturally, nationally and in other ways contextual and often specific. As existing cross-cultural research or comparison into everyday life in homes has revealed the ways people live in homes, use space, organize their lives, conceptualize and give value to different elements of materials, dirt, cleanliness and social relationships can vary immensely (see Dovey 1999; Miller 2001; Pink 2004). It would be naïve to think that the digital material environments of home that we now inhabit and that will continue to change into the future would be any different. In this section we draw on our own and others' existing work to highlight a set of key entry points into comprehending how the digital materiality of home plays out, and in doing so identify these as themes that need to be accounted for as we move on into changing (but as yet unknown in terms of their specific forms) configurations of digital materiality in future homes.

One of the core findings of our research has been to show how digital elements become part of the environment of home, in ways similar to our interpretation of how laundry and lighting become part of the materiality and atmosphere of environments of home discussed above. Conventionally in media and communication studies, digital media have been studied for their communication uses and for their content. Media anthropologists and those media scholars whose work connects with anthropology have also treated media technologies as a form of material culture and have generally understood such technologies as things that will be appropriated (e.g. see Horst and Miller 2012) within existing ways of life and environments. However our work has pushed these understandings further to consider how digital technologies and media are part of the experiential environment of home. This means considering how they are experienced, and used as part of what we have referred to in the last section as the atmosphere of home. In this section we discuss three aspects of this: the notion of digital technologies and media as presence in the home; how the affordances and qualities digital technologies and media participate in the constitution of atmospheres of home; and the place of the everyday routines of home in the making of these digital–material–atmospheres.

In Chapter 1 we introduced the concept of media presence; the idea that everyday life in homes is not only saturated, as media scholars have argued, by media content but also by the presence and potentiality of digital technologies and media, those that are waiting to be activated, or that will produce alerts. As we have argued elsewhere (Pink and Leder Mackley 2013), this means that digital technologies and media are entangled with what it means to live in homes, and are part of how we experience and anticipate their unfolding (see Chapter 2). As developed in the LEEDR project, the concept of media presence was used to describe a context where households had their own Wi-Fi connections, always 'on' at home, where most households had multiple digital technologies and devices, and where standby modes were often used, meaning that technologies were often not 'off', even when not being actively engaged with. It should also be noted that what is regarded as being on and off can also be contextual, and when the house is generally 'off', some appliances can be 'on'. For instance Alan, one participant who was happy that the main electrical appliances in his home were switched off at night, did not appear to find it relevant that the Wi-Fi, his radio alarm clock or his charging phone were all actually using electricity during the night, thus creating a particular form of media presence. In different cultural contexts media presence might moreover stand for different configurations. For example, in contexts where the primary mode of accessing the internet is not via home Wi-Fi connections, but via smart phones, different forms and intensities of media presence will be experienced and achieved. The concept of media presence, we argue, is significant in that it represents a particular way of being with media that has come to predominate, albeit in different ways, in the present. The ways that people have developed to engage with and to categorize different aspects of its presence are important to attend to since they may be indicative of the principles through which people will engage with differently digital homes, which in the future might carry with them the possibilities offered by smart technologies.

In the previous section we emphasized a focus on atmospheres of home, through the example of the role that lighting technologies and their uses play in their constitution. Digital technologies and media can also play a key role in the ways atmospheres of home are constituted, and indeed the example of media presence discussed in the previous paragraph can be seen as an element of such atmospheres. In existing work we have explored how atmospheres of home have been constituted through the use of lighting and media in the bedtime routines that we have discussed in Chapter 1, as part of the temporalities and transition moments of home (Pink and Leder Mackley 2016). We have also considered how the sound, light, thermal affordances, as well as visual aspects of digital media content and technology, are implicated in the making of atmospheres of home (Pink, Leder Mackley and Moroşanu 2015). The example of our research on UK households demonstrates well how multiple media uses can form part of the ongoingly changing process of the making of atmosphere of home. For instance, (as described in Pink, Leder Mackley and Moroşanu 2015) for the Ashton family (Barbara, her husband and their school-age children), the atmosphere of their large and light kitchen was partially constituted through media. Barbara described to us how

in the morning, [the kitchen TV] gets switched on by my husband, because I forget, I wouldn't turn the telly on, but he likes the news, and the children like the news, so if the telly's on, it's always the news ... and then it gets put on when Amy plays on the Wii. ... And then sometimes I'll put the TV on if I'm cooking tea ... and then it will stay on all evening until we leave this room, and the kids have gone to bed.

The Ashton's living room also was reconfigured materially, sensorially and emotionally in the making of an atmosphere of 'cosiness' sometimes in the evenings. As we write elsewhere:

FIGURE. 3.7 *The Ashtons' living room TV and sofa. © LEEDR.*

Materiality, media, sensory and emotional experience and atmosphere again came together in Barbara's account of the 'cosy' sitting room – which was constituted through carefully selected material objects, including the fireplace, carpet, fluffy rug (which also hid dirt from the fire), a large white modular sofa, the television being on, as well as the sense of being together with family. Evenings often ended in the sitting room, with the door half-closed so the dog could move in and out while curtailing the flow of noise from the TV upstairs to the children's bedrooms. The family sometimes re-designed the room for an evening by changing into their pyjamas, bringing down duvets and turning the sofa into a gigantic bed for everyone to lay on, watching TV with fireplace lit. Thus demonstrating the ongoingness of the atmospheres associated with this room, as the family's mudane forms of improvisation made and remade its atmosphere replete with sensory and emotional affordances through forms of temporal and material organisation. (Pink, Leder Mackley and Moroşanu 2015)

Another way of thinking about how people experience the environment of home through digital technologies and media involves engaging the concept of play. In the design research context, Dixon, Mitchell and Harker have found that women would play 'cheesy' mobile phone games at home for comfort, often to work through emotions (Dixon, Mitchell and Harker 2003). More recently, as part of their digital ethnography research about the uses of mobile media in households in Melbourne Sarah Pink, Larissa Hjorth, Heather Horst, Josh Nettheim and Genevieve Bell have investigated how playful modes of engagement with mobile media also contribute to the atmosphere of home. This work, because it takes as its analytical entry point into the home a different concept – that of play – demonstrates a different approach to learning about atmospheres of home ethnographically. Here, developing the concept of 'ambient play' with the wider environment of home, Hjorth and Ingrid Richardson have discussed how 'ambient play contextualizes the game within broader processes of sociality and embodied media practices, and is essential to the corporeality of play whereby play in, and outside, the game space reflects broader cultural nuances and phenomena' (2014: 60). Pink et al. develop this further to argue that while 'engaging in ambient play is part of the way that people may experience being in the world', if we also understand 'play and use of mobile devices' as situated, then, 'because the use of mobile devices also occurs as part of or in between other activities, the ambience of digital play can be seen as part of the wider atmospheres of everyday life, and indeed as impacting on how everyday life feels – emotionally and sensorially – as it is played out in different digital-material environments' (Pink et al. 2017). Taking this perspective allows us to consider how digital play therefore takes place in the digital materiality of homes and becomes part of the way they are experienced, and moreover, as they argue: 'Mobile games are not simply entertainment media, but they are part of the process through which our participants make everyday environments in ongoing ways at the interface between work and home' (Pink et al. 2017). The implication of this for the discussion here is that if we are to understand how home is constituted as an environment, it is essential for us to attend to the everyday ways that home and the possibilities that people have to feel sensorially and emotionally in homes are made through everyday digital media practices. For example, one of the participants in the *Locating the Mobile* project discussed by Pink et al., called Amanda, described how she would

> play *Solitaire* on her phone, which she kept with her when working with her laptop on the bed on her laptop, 'not all the time' but rather when she experienced anxiety at home, as such as part of the way of constituting the way being at home feels to her. Amanda explained that 'I get anxious. I have anxiety issues and I find that it calms me down, quite a bit.' (Pink et al. 2017)

Here we see how the participant's tactile and emotional engagement with the technology was not an isolated instance of digital play, but that it was specifically situated in a context of working from home, with a particular configuration of other technologies, and a specific site (the bed) within the home. If, like many games researchers, we are to consider play to be one of the key ways that people engage with their digital material worlds, following processes of digital play as they interweave with other elements of everyday life in homes offers a useful prism through which to understand how digital technologies and specific modes of engagement with them form part of the ways people make homes. This, we propose, is significant in relation to the question of how to design for and with digital material homes and the people who live in them.

As we discussed in Chapter 2, the routines and rhythms of everyday life are part of the ways in which home is constituted, and ongoingly made, renewed and transformed. Digital technologies and media play an important role in these processes, not only in creating a sense of home, or feeling of home in terms of atmosphere, but also in terms of making senses of feeling at home or of familiarity. Recent research has demonstrated how digital media are implicated in the making of atmospheres of home in a number of ways. One example of this concerns the generation of a sense of feeling comfortable when being away from home, or when a person, who is normally close to us in our home life, is away from home. Existing research into the use of digital media for communications across transnationally based migrant households (e.g. Madianou and Miller 2012), and intergenerational uses of social media (Hjorth et al. 2015; Pink Sinanan et al. 2016), has demonstrated how the digital social presence of those people who are absent physically is important. As the examples discussed above in this section also show, the routine and mundane elements of everyday life underpin the ways in which people use media throughout their days at home in order to make, remake or transform the feel of home and the ways that they feel *in* their homes. This might be at bedtime, at meal times, within working from home processes, or at other moments in the day. Such uses of media are also sometimes contested, as we take up further in the next chapter through our focus on how we might account for human activity in homes. Digital technologies are inextricably implicated in how our sensory and emotional forms of well-being are invested in and derived from our relationships with the digital material environments of home.

Implications: Designing for the digital–material–atmospheric home

In this chapter we have shown how by approaching the home as an environment we are able to come to understand how it is constituted and experienced as material, digital and as atmospheric – that is as an everyday site that is sensory and emotional. While we divided up the discussion into three categories of, or elements of, environments – the material, atmospheric and digital – these are not, in fact, separate from each other, as the discussion has shown. Rather they are categories or concepts that we can use to design and to understand research, that is, they are ways of dividing up aspects of the environment of home, so that they can be studied, worked on or intervened with.

We argue that design ethnography research into the home cannot afford not to account for the home as a material, sensory and affective, and digital environment. Each of the areas we have discussed in this chapter has already been brought to bear in a relationship with design: through the material culture studies strand in the design anthropology literature (Clarke 2010); through HCI and digital design (Dourish and Bell 2011); and through sensory design for architecture (Palasmaa 1994) and the idea of designing atmospheres (Edensor and Sumartojo 2015). As we have seen in the preceding sections of this chapter, as they engage with these material, digital and sensory/affective/atmospheric elements of home, people navigate, appropriate and improvise as the relations between themselves and their homes are ongoingly depending on the contingencies of whatever else is happening around them. Just as we have shown in Chapter 2 that the question of what will happen next is always contingent, the ways that the digital–material–sensory environments in which we live are configured also emerge from and as a contingent world. This is not to say there were no patterns in our findings: when people share cultural, material, digital and sensory environments, they are often likely to come up against similar challenges and to develop similar (but not the same) ways of coping with these. To be able to effectively design for change in homes, however, we need to be able to comprehend how such processes play out, and how, as emphasized in the last chapter, they are implicated in the anticipatory modes of living in homes.

The examples discussed in this chapter collectively reveal the home as a dynamic environment where materialities, technologies and intangible things and processes are continually flowing, moving and changing. They combine in different ways to constitute home as an experiential environment. Yet, as we have also shown, home in this scenario is not a perfect or necessarily coherent configuration. Things do not always work in the way they were designed to – things break, processes get broken. Solutions are improvised, but sometimes the solutions to one problem create other forms of breakage. That is, the home cannot be seen as a 'system', because it is 'messy' (Dourish and Bell 2011; Law 2004). Indeed, while here we have focused on what people do to ensure home 'feels right', often it does not. The home can therefore be conceptualized as being in a state of potentially feeling right, or with the possibility of feeling right.

How will future homes emerge as generative of particular ways of feeling, that are sensory and emotional and that are the ongoing outcomes of the digital, material and human relations that constitute them? And how can we play a role in determining that such future homes will be increasingly environmentally sustainable, or that they will be sites of human well-being and happiness? The question for designing in/for/with homes, in this sense, is: How can interventions be made to enable this process? While this is an abstract question, when set in the context of the more specific one of how we might understand and design for the digital materiality of the future home, the implications are clearer. We propose that a focus on the atmospheres of the digital material home offers a key framework through which to consider what future homes are being designed for. As noted in Chapter 1 the future possible smart home has been much discussed. However, as the discussion in this chapter implies, the digital material homes that people live in are not determined by technological possibilities, but rather by how people engage with and how they feel in relation to the specific configurations of material, technological and sensory configurations that come about. Therefore, as Strengers has argued (2016), we cannot predict how people will live and if they will live in a more environmentally sustainable way in smart homes, or with smart home technologies. Rather to be able to assist people in living sustainably, we need to comprehend the principles through which they already live, with and through existing digital materialities. We pursue this question further in the next chapter through a focus on human activity and movement in the home.

4

Activity and movement

This chapter focuses on what people *do* in the home and explores how a concept of movement can fruitfully be engaged to study this. The question of how to categorize what people do into units that can be effectively researched, analysed and reported on has taken various forms in academic theory and scholarship. The categories that have been commonly used to describe what people do in homes in academic research, including those such as practices and behaviours, tend to be tightly bound to particular bodies of social theory and the academic disciplinary debates that they are associated with. This is always limiting in the context of change-making since the way such concepts are subsequently used can often have more to do with critical debates between and within academic disciplines, than with their utility for understanding the possibilities of what might happen next/in the future. Therefore, we argue that for an interventional, change-making and design-oriented approach to ethnography, an alternative and more open concept for understanding human activity is needed.

We propose that in the context of researching and designing for and with people in the home, conceptualizing *doing* as activity that happens as people move forward – both through the world and through their lives – creates such an open concept. A concept of *movement*, we suggest, offers a design ethnography approach to the home as a way to approach the world as processual and continually changing, while also accounting for the place of people in this world. This does not infer that other concepts are not useful, in that we will continue to use those, such as practices, behaviours and others, but that by relinquishing these constraints to a concept of movement, we are able to understand the ways people live in their homes from another perspective that enriches and guides our ways of researching and designing with/for homes in new ways. This means we can therefore acknowledge that people and things are ongoingly moving through their environments (homes), and that they are also in various different ways actively engaged in making interventions in the environment of home. A movement-oriented approach also accommodates the arguments we have made for a consideration of the temporality of home in Chapter 2 and for the conceptualization of the home as an ongoingly changing digital, material, sensory, emotional and atmospheric environment, introduced in Chapter 3. In putting the concept of movement at the centre of our discussion in this chapter, we also consider how we might engage such an understanding in order to develop collaborations between designers, ethnographers and people living out their lives in their homes for the making of sustainable everyday futures. All of whom we understand to be similarly in movement.

Movement as an approach

Movement has in recent years become a significant concept in the social sciences and humanities, reaching across disciplines including human geography (Massey 2005) and anthropology (e.g. Ingold 2007, 2010). These fundamental works, and the literatures they have inspired, enable us to focus on movement as a key factor in the processes through which everyday life contexts are constituted, and can be applied to our understanding of how homes are ongoingly made (Pink 2012). This emphasis on human movement, as well as the movement of things, has become all the more important in the more immediate past through the increasing ubiquity of mobile media, which are now a key element of the way in which we experience the digital material worlds we live in (see for example Goggin and Hjorth 2014). This has led to a focus of research about mobile media, which includes a vibrant strand in digital ethnography (e.g. Hjorth and Pink 2014; Horst 2014a, b, 2016) as it crosses over between anthropology and media studies and provides a background from which to consider how human movement and activity, and mobile media are co-implicated in the constitution of everyday life in the home.

Ethnographic approaches are particularly suited to researching through movement because they acknowledge the need to engage with others as they follow their routes through the world. Ethnographically we might follow people, things or processes, accompany them and as such trace the ways they proceed. Design, and other applied disciplines that seek to make interventions towards change, likewise, we argue, can benefit from working through a concept of movement. While ethnographers can trace the routes people have already taken through the world, right up to the moment that they slip over into their futures without us, designers and applied researchers need to seek ways to continue with them, taking into the future the interventions that we propose to make with them. An emphasis on movement therefore brings to the fore a set of issues similar to those that we have discussed in relation to the temporalities of ethnography, design and home. The point is that we need to understand how people move through the digital material home, in order that we should be able to determine how they might be best accompanied by those things and processes that will be needed in the future, as they move on with or without us into the future that is not yet known.

We next discuss how existing approaches to human activity in the home have developed, and connect these to an approach that puts movement at the centre of its analysis.

The study of human activity in the home

Because the home is a key site for intervention – not only by designers, but also by agencies such as health care workers (Taylor and Donnelly 2006; Pink et al. 2015), social workers (Ferguson 2009, 2010), as well as being a context for domestic work (Law 2001; Pratt 1999; Smith 2011) and for working from home (Hanson and Pratt 1998; Dyck et al. 2005), there are a number of existing approaches to understanding how people live in the home and the kinds of activities they undertake there. Such work has also been inflected by various key themes in the social sciences and humanities over several decades. These include a focus on the gendered nature of human activity in the home, often through a discussion of housework (see Pink 2004 for a review of this literature), and as we have noted in Chapter 1, the problematic or darker side of everyday gender and power relations has also been emphasized by scholars of home in a range of disciplines, notably human geography (e.g. Blunt and Dowling 2006; Brickell 2012, 2014).

Social scientists have tended to take a series of discipline-specific approaches to understanding what people do in their homes. We have outlined some of these ways of understanding the home according to disciplinary interests in Chapter 1, and these are generally also coherent with the ways that activity in the home is understood. Here we write about these selectively, and in relation to their relevance for our focus on movement. In anthropology the work of Danny Miller, concerning what people *do* in their homes, has brought to the fore an important emphasis on the home as a site for the constitution of identity. Miller's research with people in their homes has tended to be based on visiting people in their homes, rather than actually engaging with them in activity in the home, but nevertheless offers significant insights into the idea of the home as a site of human activity. The material culture studies approach, which Miller shares with Alison Clarke (2001), Adam Drazin (2001), Horst (2006, 2011) and others, is also useful because it brings to the fore the incompleteness of processes of home, discussed in Chapter 2. It is also significant because due to its focus on materiality, it reminds us that people and things move through the world together and suggests how they cluster and re-cluster. In sociology there has also been a focus on research in homes, which has often taken a social practice theory perspective (e.g. Shove 2003; Shove et al. 2007). While as noted in Chapter 1 (and see Pink et al. 2014) a practice-centred approach is limited, particularly when it is based on interviews (see Pink 2012), it has also been usefully engaged in work that seeks to follow the actual activities of people in homes. For example, Lydia Martens has used CCTV camera recordings, made in collaboration with people in their homes, in order to document and subsequently analyse everyday activities – social practices – in kitchens as they happened (Martens 2012). Yolande Strengers has undertaken research, which has involved her in asking people to take her around their homes, while she has photographed (Strengers 2013; Maller and Strengers 2013) in order to interrogate people's existing social practices in homes.

In common, these approaches have all been concerned with either the outcomes of prior activity in the home or with actual performances of activity in the home. This includes DIY minor work on the home (Miller 2001; Shove et al. 2007), and reorganization of the home (Garvey 2001) as well as everyday tasks in the kitchen or bathroom (Martens 2014; Maller and Strengers 2013), or both (Pink 2004). Our own work has also been concerned with understanding what our participants have done in the past, and how they represent in collaborative encounters with us what they 'usually do'. In the LEEDR project we took two perspectives on studying movement in the home: by mapping it from above and by tracing it as it goes through. Mapping from above offers a participant-generated cross-sectional view of how people use space and where intensities of use might lie as people move around to different areas of homes in different moments in the day (as discussed below). Going through the home, in contrast, creates a line through the home, enabling us to see what it is that is collected or changed on the way, and how people improvise as they encounter challenges, events, people, things and activities on their way through. However when undertaking research that seeks to go beyond simply understanding what people have done, and to intervene in what they do in the future, we need to be able to go beyond the specificity of what has happened already, and to acknowledge that part of our research field also encompasses the question of what might happen next, or what might usually happen next.

While superficially it seems obvious to claim that people live according to regular routines or rhythms, and that they repeat the things they do each day or each week, this claim, in fact, is problematic. If we take the starting point that we live as part of an ongoingly changing environment as outlined in Chapter 3, in such a context, people perform something similar each time but do not repeat exactly the same activity, neither do they perform it in exactly the same place. As the geographer Doreen Massey (2005) pointed out, we can never go back to a place or time we have previously inhabited. Such places disperse and likewise we only ever do anything once. When performed again, it is never the same action, and it will never be performed in exactly the same circumstances in the future. Even if these differences might be barely perceptible, the impossibility of absolute or complete replication is important to keep in mind as a background understanding when considering what people 'do' since this point puts the generalizability of what people do into question. It also reminds us that we need, as researchers, to attend to the details of how activities have changed over time, and to reflect on what this might mean for how they will continue to change. Theoretical concepts that have been used traditionally in the social sciences are often not adequate for such tasks, precisely because in existing anthropological or sociological literatures they have always been used to describe human activities that have *always already happened*. Indeed we could argue that such concepts as those of a 'social practice' or an appropriation of material culture have been developed in the social sciences to account for things that are in the past. They are 'after-the-event' concepts that can be applied to things that have already happened, but that might be less useful for applying to what has not happened yet. The reason for this is that once a social science researcher gets to the stage of analysis, she or he is able to divide up the accounts of the world that has been encountered into units that can be interpreted. It is not a world in movement that is any longer being dealt with, but one that has been stopped and deliberated temporally situated in the past, for a range of academic, ethical and methodological reasons. Concepts that are used as such to analyse past events that have been (inevitably falsely) divided up for the convenience of analysis do not represent the actual contingencies and complexities of futures as they unfold. Instead, they provide 'unreal' categories that may not actually exist in futures and moreover may lack a focus towards the future, that is, they do not have an orientation that always accounts for what will possibly happen next, but that we do not yet know about. In some disciplines, however, anticipating what might happen next or how to make interventions is essential.

A good example of applied research field that takes the home as one of its sites of investigation and possible intervention is social work research. The social work researcher and scholar Harry Fergusson's work is particularly interesting in this context because he has developed a focus on how service users' homes become (often complex and difficult) experiential sites for social workers to navigate, physically and emotionally. Connecting with our discussion in Chapter 3, Ferguson also shows how the atmospheres of home are part of the environments that social workers carry out their work in. For

Ferguson, in discussing the home visit, which is a fundamental element of the everyday work of many social workers, and particularly in the context of child protection work, which he discusses, the concepts of 'movement, adventure, atmosphere and emotion' (2010: 1102) are important. He is concerned with movement in particular because

> social work always involves potential movement, as mobility does not always happen when it should ... when service users refuse entry to homes or overtly or covertly constrain the worker's movements; or when workers do not assert their need to be mobile when in the presence of the child and family and restrict their own movements. This can happen on the street, in the high-rise housing block, as well as in the key site of the service user's home. (2010: 1100–1)

He argues that 'the necessity to walk around rooms and homes to establish the wellbeing of children has to be taken as a standard of good social work' and suggests that conversely, 'when the worker does not move either because they do not realise its importance or because their movement is blocked by service users' tactics, this immobilisation places the child at (higher) risk' (2010: 1112). As Ferguson's work shows, in order to understand other people's ways of being in their homes, as researchers, as well as practitioners in applied fields, being able to move with people and through homes is an important basis for our knowing. It suggests that the immobilized researcher likewise is constrained, and that designing for people who are understood as anything but mobile themselves is delimited in the same way.

In Chapter 1 we discussed how a theory of human improvisation can offer us a way to understand how people live in and navigate the environment of home. The approach we develop in this chapter also understands people as ongoingly reinventing aspects of their everyday life activities and emphasizes how they do this in subtle but actual ways as they move through the world. Approaching the home through movement offers a category, which is open to, and retains a space for, not knowing what will happen next. It allows us to evade the use of an objectified or objective model of a set of bounded activities that people perform but instead supports the search for a way into knowing about how human activity is part of the 'flow' of everyday life. While, as Pink (2012) has discussed, this creates philosophical issues and questions about the possibility of ever capturing and being able to describe such activity, for the purposes of bringing together design and ethnography, there is another practical issue which suggests the need for an approach that is open to the future in this way. This is because to be able to intervene in the world we need to be able to find entry points into everyday life, together with participants, which will enable them to take changes with them, or make changes, as they move on into futures that we may not be closely co-implicated in. The approach we propose offers an alternative to seeing these activities as concrete practices – such as 'the laundry', 'showering', 'cooking' or using media. Instead we are interested in examining how things that fit into those categories get 'picked up' and carried along by people as they move through the world. In fact as our research has revealed, because activities such as these tend to be dispersed and get mixed up along the messy routes that people take through the everyday, a narrative of human movement also enables us to understand better their situatedness in relation to each other and their mutual contingencies.

Moving through the home in practice

In this and the following sections we approach moving through the home from two perspectives. First, here we return to our discussions of bedtime routines and lighting, developed in Chapters 2 and 3, in order to show how these routines of movement pull together elements of different everyday practices of home. Our point here is to show that moving through the home can be treated both in the context of research design and analytically as a 'thread' through which to gain understandings of how people live in their homes and how different elements of everyday life are bound together in the forward moving dynamics through which the complex ecologies of things, persons and processes become configured into and disperse from clusters of intensity within the flow of the everyday. Second, in the following sections we focus in on the use of everyday 'practices' as entry points into other people's world. However, unlike much existing research that tends to be interested in understanding the dynamics of these practices themselves, we focus on how we might understand them as situated within routines of movement through the home, which involve the flows of people, things, fresh air, warmth, energy, water and many other tangible and intangible elements of home. To demonstrate the latter we next focus on the example of cooking-related activities.

In our articles and presentations one of the key activities in the home that we have discussed based on our own research is the way people move around in their homes at night-time on their way to bed. Here we bring this example to the fore again for a particular purpose, to emphasize how movement through the home as part of specific routines can offer us ways to understand how key sets of activities are pulled together into routines, so that they become inextricable from each other. As we have seen in Chapter 2 such routines are forward moving in that they are future-focused and involve transitions into the night-time, which are also orientated towards ensuring that people can move on into the next day. This discussion also picks up some key themes from Chapter 3, in that we see how transition to the night-time home is also an activity in the making and experience of a particular atmosphere of home, while moving through.

In Chapter 3, Figure 3.6, we show a still image from one of our LEEDR videos (video 28 at www.energyanddigitalliving.com), captured from a night-time routine re-enactment. This image is of an area of the participant's living room before the lights were switched off. This particular participant's downstairs routine was quite typical of that of a family household with animals and children. Stephen, who lived with his wife and youngest son (with occasional visits from adult children), began his re-enactment in the living room. He showed us how he moved through the room, switching off lights and technologies, and opening the door into the garden to let the dog out and back in again. He followed a route through the living area into the kitchen where he told us that his and his wife's laptops, which were open for work on the table, would be closed down and put away in their laptop bags, the dishwasher would be turned on, they would get a glass of water, say goodnight to the dog and then, he told us, everything would be off and locked and they would go up to bed. About thirty minutes before, if he had remembered, he would have gone upstairs to switch on the electric blanket; if he hadn't, then he or his wife would switch it on, to heat up the bed a bit while they were in the bathroom. Once in bed he would read, and he claimed his wife would be looking at her emails, and both would plug their phones in to charge. Then finally they would both switch off their bedside lights.

In our LEEDR research it became clear that most participants followed similar routines of movement. They thus created routes through their homes, covering doors, windows, lights letting pets out and in, electronic devices, going into the bathroom and finally getting into bed. These were clearly culturally specific ways of ending the day or evening; however, we also note that these ways of moving through the home at night-time were contingent on participants having access to particular social, material and infrastructural elements of home. As we discuss in the final section of this chapter, human movement is also always contextual and contingent in this way and needs to be understood in relation to the movement of other things and processes.

Cooking as movement

On the surface we might consider that each activity that is undertaken in the home – such as cooking, laundry or showering – could be seen as a separate unit or practice. However ethnographic research with people in their homes can reveal the limitations of this model, and simultaneously in dialogue with theory, propose alternative ways of understanding and situating such activity. For example, one of the LEEDR 'everyday activity' (or 'in-practice') studies sought to explore how energy use was implicated in relation to kitchen activities, specifically cooking and cleaning. For the purposes of our visits, we momentarily approached cooking as a broadly bounded activity; in a practical sense, participants were accomplishing the task of bringing together a range of ingredients to produce a meal that would feed the family. There was, generally speaking, a beginning and an end to this food preparation. Yet, these activities were also interwoven with others, and thus the concept of movement, as it emerged from our participant encounters and as we subsequently pursued it, allowed us to follow the flow of activities within that more open and complex mesh of doings. We asked to visit participants when they were preparing an everyday meal, which was often taken to be the evening meal, although we also attended to breakfast, lunch and snack times. What was immediately apparent with these family households was that, although participants often aimed to get together over a family meal, bedtime routines, work and extracurricular activities affected who would be available for food at any one time. In most households, the kitchen was actively designed and used as a family hub (cf. Bech-Danielsen 2012 for a historical discussion of changes in kitchen design), a space where people and things would come together in and pass through. Subsequently, and as has been noted in other writings on the home (e.g. Nippert-Eng 2008), the kitchen was not just a space for cooking or eating, but also for work, play and sometimes the laundry. Media were increasingly part of the kitchen environment, with several families using a TV in the kitchen and one participant family in particular leaving the kitchen radio on all day, providing a visual and, in the latter case, auditory landscape that accompanied, invited or prohibited people's movement through the home. Similarly, mobile devices accompanied people into the kitchen or found their temporary home on kitchen surfaces. The kitchen was also a focal point for movement through the home with regard to tea- and coffee-making facilities, with the making of hot beverages often accompanying or intersecting with other activities. Conversely, other areas of the home were implicated in what would usually be delineated as kitchen or cooking practices, including the garden, which has been discussed in other literature in terms of its relationship to the English home (Chevalier 1995, 1998). For example, in the case of Andrea and her family, dinner preparation often started in the garden, as shown in Figure 4.1.

When Kerstin visited, Andrea's route through the garden initially traced back gardening utensils which she had left at the far end when doing gardening work earlier in the day. She told Kerstin that she had a general idea of the kinds of vegetables that would be ready to eat and that she used them 'when I know it fits in', demonstrating how temporality (see Chapter 2) is also experienced sensorially in the knowledge of how vegetables grow in the garden. Similarly, Andrea spoke of her tacit knowledge of the contents of fridges and freezers, with a sense of when things needed to be used up for cooking. After cutting off some courgettes, Andrea dug deep into a soil-filled container to retrieve some potatoes which she proceeded to wash in the utility room. The latter served as a connection between the inside and the outside of the home; it was where shoes got changed, hands and vegetables got washed, and it also contained the washing machine (thus forming part of the laundry routes through the home). As Andrea filled a small plastic bowl with water, she told Kerstin that she would usually adjust the water heat, for her hands not to get too cold during the cleaning process. This was less of an issue when her hands were already warm, as they were on the hot day Kerstin visited.

Andrea had already put some chicken into the oven and was now preparing potatoes and a variety of vegetables to go with it. The courgettes went into a ratatouille, although Andrea knew that her daughters would not eat the latter and so she also cooked green beans. She used her hands to rip off the ends of the beans and handled a knife to cut the vegetables, including courgettes and aubergines. Throughout the cooking process, Andrea had to navigate different areas of the kitchen, specifically moving between a kitchen isle, the oven cooker, the fridge, an ingredient cupboard, other utensil shelves and the sink (which, incidentally, was situated on the far side of the kitchen, at some distance from the kettle and cooker), in order to make 'cooking' happen. At the same time, she tidied, reorganized and cleaned the kitchen (although the bulk of washing up was left for her husband to sort out), and she interacted with family members who were passing through. One way of approaching Andrea's movement through the kitchen is to map it and, for instance, consider the kinds of 'affordances' (cf. Gibson 1977) that kitchen design and positioning of tools and gadgets invited or restricted. Interaction designers have previously mapped movement through the kitchen accordingly, at the same time as attending to the ways in which hands and bodies were used during the cooking process, with attention towards the kinds of digital interactions that might be possible (e.g. Paay et al. 2015). This kind of mapping of activity can indeed reveal interesting insights into intersections between activities, people and their environment, and intensities of movement and activity, also in relation to time. In fact, we might consider how new products, services or technologies might facilitate or hinder movement, offer different avenues for movement, interrupt movement, allow things to move or encourage people and things to move together.

Yet our work of following participants with the camera and attending to their sensory experiences also alerted us to how people's movement and activities 'made' and were constitutive of the environment, as discussed in Chapter 3.

FIGURE 4.1 *Food preparation begins and ends in the garden for this family of four. The above images offer a way into the sensory-experiential and tactile aspects of a process that is accomplished through the movements of people and things.* © *LEEDR.*

For instance, one issue that came to the fore through engaging with participants' activities in and around the kitchen was how it was a space in which participants had to negotiate different flows of often intangible things, like cooking smells, steam, light and lighting, or sounds, such as the noise of extractor fans (we address more of these below). In Andrea's case, the door to the utility room and garden was left open for a breeze on what was an exceptionally hot day, whereas she repeatedly shut the door to the rest of the house, in order to prevent chicken smells from entering the above bedrooms; she generally avoided the use of the extractor fan because of its noise, although she put it on when Kerstin visited, in the hope that it might remove some heat from the kitchen. We were first alerted to these kinds of negotiation of flows when visiting a household with a partially deaf family member for whom it was important to avoid distracting noises, such as music and fans, while generating sufficient sources of light to be able to lip read (Pink and Leder Mackley 2014a). This is the kind of ethnographic insight that often emerges during the research process, when demonstrated through an encounter where, as in this case, the participant was able to show and articulate the complexity of the context she was involved in. On following it up we realized that this example had given us a key to investigating how such combinations of flows were detected and managed by participants across a range of other contexts and situations in the home. This thus led us to conceptualize householders as playing the role of directors of flows.

At the same time, our focus on movement, along with a general interest in participants' sensorial worlds, revealed acts of everyday improvisation as people sensed their way through kitchen and activities. For instance, Andrea told us how she would use the remaining heat in her turned off oven to warm up plates before serving, something which was not necessary on a hot summer day but which she would frequently do during the winter. Incidentally, the weather was relevant for both what she cooked and how she cooked, and for where she placed food and ingredients, for instance to keep them from flies.

Similarly, as with our attention to the night-time home, we could think of the cooking process as one of transformation, transition and, thus, change. Change happened to the potatoes as they were taken from their soil, washed, cooked, served and eaten. Change happened to the garden as vegetables were removed to be processed, and change happened to the kitchen as utensils were used, and waste, heat, steam and smells were generated. Andrea's body likewise underwent changes, with hands getting dirty, washed (warmed up or cooled down), used for handling; and with her body having to acclimatize to the increasingly hot kitchen (which Andrea eventually escaped from, in order to enjoy dinner in the garden). How these movements and transitions are relevant to wider projects of change may depend on and inform specific research and design challenges. Importantly, they go beyond cooking as a bounded set of activities, and they might usefully go beyond mapping movements and activities from above, instead offering a route into a range of experiential and environmental opportunities for change.

We have hinted towards how media might become part of kitchen environments. Andrea further told us how she might use the internet to get inspiration for recipes, specifically when she knew she had to use up particular types of food. Below, we discuss in more detail how media and movement might usefully be engaged for research and design.

Digital technologies and media on the move

Earlier research about media in homes has focused on a range of areas that provide relevant background for design ethnography understandings of everyday life in the home; we do not review this extensive literature here but point to key earlier concerns with the appropriation of media and technologies, its use for the coordination of human activity and movement, or how they engage with its content, apps or platforms (e.g. to note but a few: Silverstone and Hirsch 1992; Morley 2000; Christensen and Ropke 2010; Horst 2012). These existing literatures are useful because they provide an excellent background of suggestions concerning how people live with, feel about, or derive a sense of companionship and well-being from media and digital technologies. With this in mind, however, here we propose a focus on digital media in relation to the ways that people move through the home with them. As we show below, this approach to digital media and their relationship to movement also underpins the possibilities we propose for the use of such technologies as part of digital design interventions.

Our research has shown that there are two ways in which digital technologies are implicated in how participants move around in their homes that are particularly interesting in the context of our concern with design ethnography. The first is that digital technologies tend to be dispersed around homes. Some of them have established sites in particular places in specific rooms, like wall-mounted screens or large pieces of equipment. Others are mobile but tend to be usually left in one particular place, for instance, as discussed below, examples of tablets being kept on a specific table recurred in different projects. These two types of technology tend to be those that people move *between*. Another category consists mainly of smartphones and other small mobile devices that are carried by their owner most of the time, although they tend to have specific stopping points where they are charged or sometimes left. Finally and most recently has been the emergence of wearables, used generally for self-tracking of body activity by people, but which also include technologies that can be used for communication and content, and that in the case of self-tracking technologies sometimes have social media elements.

These different categories have tended to become more apparent in different studies in relation to what the specific object of the project has been. For example, in the context of the LEEDR study we soon became aware that mobile technologies, specifically smartphones and tablets, formed part of how people experienced movement around their homes, and between homes and other locations. Participants carried their phones on them during the encounters with us or plugged them in to charge during their re-enactments of night-time routines. They also used their smartphones, as might be expected, as they went about their lives in their homes during the day. For example, one participant (see video 38 at www.energyanddigitalliving.com), when Roxana asked her when she would normally use her phone, responded that 'it's just around all the time' and went on to describe how when she had recently seen blackberries in the fields near her home and someone with her had mentioned blackberry whisky, and how when she got home, she searched for information on her phone about how to make it. Another participant showed us on video how he would look up information on his tablet while watching television. As such we can see how smartphones and tablets *accompanied* participants as they moved through their everyday lives at home, in and out of other activities and between different rooms.

We also saw how LEEDR participants moved between different digital technologies as they moved between different rooms in which they were used or kept. For instance, one participant, Lee (see video 32 at www. energyanddigitalliving.com), showed us how during his morning routine, the television would be put on in three different rooms in the house – the bedroom, kitchen and living room – during different stages of the family's activity as he and his wife prepared themselves and their toddler for work and nursery. The TV and smartphone also figured in Lee's night-time routine, in which he, like other participants, followed a familiar route through the home. Here he started his routine, on the sofa, with his cat and with the TV on. He showed us how he would then switch off the TV, and the lamp, but put the light on in the centre of the room, before walking through into the kitchen, carrying the cat, which he would let out for the night, locking the door behind it. He would then switch off the TV in the kitchen at the wall, go to the toilet and return to the living room to finish switching off the TV. Then he continued his route, up the stairs, into the bathroom, and finally into the bedroom, where he would plug his phone into charge and, if it was still on, finally switch off the TV in the bedroom. In such cases we witnessed how routines of movement through the home including those of getting ready in the morning, and of going to bed at night, were accompanied by media that were embedded in the spatiality of the home. Here media technologies

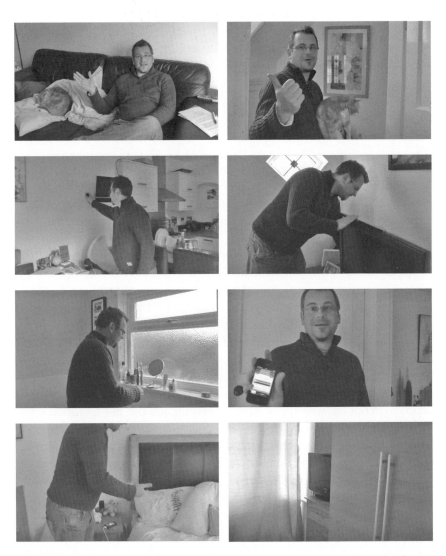

FIGURE 4.2 *Lee's night-time routine brought together digital media technologies, the cat and locking and switching activities. This created a series of contingencies that influenced the way he moved through the home. See video 32 at www. energyanddigitalliving.com. © LEEDR.*

and content were part of the environment of home discussed in Chapter 3, as well as part of the temporality of the routine as discussed in Chapter 2. The ways that media were distributed in the home tended, among the participants, to be significant in guiding the routes of movement they took around their homes.

In the context of the *Locating the Mobile* study (2014–16) which Pink was involved in, where the focus was more specifically on mobile media, examples such as that of Esther and Patrick (a migrant couple who have lived in Australia for many years) have shown how mobile devices also tend to have resting places in homes, which similarly imply the movement of persons between them. For instance, as outlined:

> Esther and Patrick are a middle-class professional couple, aged 58 and 72 respectively, with an adult daughter. We met at their home and Esther walked Sarah around the home, explaining where her devices were kept. She pointed to where she would take her phone out of her bag and leave it on the study desk in their lounge room on arriving home from work and how she always leaves her tablet on the coffee table in case her husband Patrick wants to use it. (Pink, Sinanan, Hjorth and Horst 2016)

Likewise, a participant in LEEDR kept his tablet in his study, and using it formed one of the moments in the routine of movement that he took through his home each morning (see video 31 at www.energyanddigitalliving.com). This participant showed us how he would conduct his morning routine, starting from when he got out of bed. He described how he would first go into the bathroom, then come back, get dressed and make his way downstairs, by which moment his wife might have woken up and put the television on in the bedroom to watch the news. He would then go down stairs, shouting twice to his daughters to wake them up as he passed their rooms, go into the kitchen to undertake various tasks, including making the tea, and then walking back upstairs to give his wife a cup. He would then go back downstairs to the kitchen where he then showed us how he would often take his own cup of tea and walk through across the hallway to his study where he would 'usually catch up on the day's news on the iPad' for about ten minutes, before moving across to his computer table where, he told us, he would pack his bag for the rest of the day, shout to his daughters again and then leave the house. As we see in this example, media use is part of the way people move through their homes in the routine movements of everyday life, however it is interwoven with other activities. Here the activity of reading the news on the iPad is part of the activity of having a cup of tea and is interwoven in a routine of movement that involves shouting to wake up other family members and making tea for another.

FIGURE 4.3 *This participant showed us how in the morning he stopped for a while to have a cup of tea and use his iPad as one of the activities that happened within his usual routine of movement through the home.* © LEEDR.

Within Sarah Pink and John Postill's research with Indonesian students in Melbourne, we also saw how smartphones became part of other everyday routines of movement. In this case the researchers were particularly interested in the relationship between smartphones and laundry and learned how participants had, once they moved to Melbourne, started to use smartphone weather apps in relation to both their own movement and the movement of their laundry items – by checking to make sure it would not rain before hanging laundry outdoors and to determine what they would wear as they moved out of home and went out to the university. As Pink and Postill (2016) outline:

> Using a washing machine is also embedded in everyday routines and environments, and these are also emergent as people begin to live in new ways in new localities. Retno described how while waiting for the machine to finish she would cook or read a book. Like Ratih, Retno used a weather app on her iPhone, which she would check before hanging out the laundry as well as before choosing the clothes she would wear that day. Once she had washed her clothes in the morning and there was a cloud and it rained in the day, so she had to wash her underwear again. She told us that the weather in Yogyakarta is also unpredictable like in Melbourne, and that she typically checks for updates by the hour. This habitual checking points to an overlooked dimension of digital technologies: while there is an almost obsessive academic interest in 'social media', there is significantly less attention paid to its mediating role in non-social interactions with our

physical environment, in this case with the weather. This growing use of non-social, environmental apps in everyday life is also part of migrant experience. (Pink and Postill 2016)

Here we get a sense of how the participants wove their way through the new environment they had encountered, by using smartphone apps. Their domestic tasks, and getting ready at home to go out involved this digital material engagement which entailed both sensing what Ingold (2010) has called the 'weather world' and referring to their digital context. To explain such ways of moving through the world with digital media, Pink and Hjorth (2012) have developed the concept of 'digital wayfaring' also building on Ingold's concept of the wayfarer, who weaves their way through the world in ways that are attentive to the environments that she or he passes through, rather than being directly transported (Ingold 2007). While used primarily in existing work to describe how people travel outside the home, this concept can also be used to consider the ways that we move around at home, interweaving digital and material elements of our homes as we go.

Finally, we note the increasing use of digital self-tracking technologies and how these are also becoming part of our lives in our homes. While self-tracking is also thought of primarily as something that is part of outdoor activity monitoring, it is in fact also becoming a key element of how people live in homes. In some cases this might engender increased movement in the home – for example if a person decides to go up and down their stairs a few times to increase their step count. However, perhaps more significant to consider is the use of sleep monitors, heart monitors, digital scales and calorie counters as people move around their homes as part of their everyday life activities. The wearable technologies not only move with people so that they can be used by them but they track activity as they go, creating a digital trace of this bodily activity. While self-tracking technologies are not usually considered a domestic technology, we argue that in the context of research into everyday life in the home, they ought to be accounted for as part of the ecology of media technologies that configure in the home. Wearables, which are the mobile devices that accompany us on our bodies as we move through our homes, are linked or synched to smart phone apps, or other computing technologies, which (as for the examples of digital technologies in the home discussed above in this section) may or may not be mobile within the home or taken out of it. Indeed, as Pink has found in her research on self-tracking in everyday life, self-tracking technologies can be part of how people 'play' with technology in everyday life, as well as forming part of the routines of everyday life in the home (and out of it). For instance as people check their data at certain moments in the day, and synch or upload data as part of the

FIGURE 4.4 *A participant in the Sensing, Shaping, Sharing project shows his self-tracking data. © Sarah Pink.*

routines of getting up in the morning, arriving at home after exercising or, at other moments in the day.

Digital technologies, fixed, portable or wearable, are part of our everyday lives, but significantly they also are part of the ways in which we move around in our everyday lives. In this role they are often seen as technologies or means through which to make interventions towards 'behaviour change' – such as through the delivery of SMS or other alerts towards healthy living. As discussed elsewhere, that, however, is not the only, and probably not the best, way to engage with the possibility for interventions in everyday life through digital technologies. Rather, if as we have shown in the previous section, movement is one of the ways that we engage with our homes, and how we interweave the various activities we have undertaken in our homes, the more interesting direction for scholarship and practice in this domain is to start to consider how we might engage digital technologies to create interventions in collaboration with people as they move through, and how they might use these technologies in ways that in the future are beneficial to processes of change-making through everyday life.

Non-human movement through the home

Movement in and through the home involves 'things' as well as people, this includes material objects such as those discussed already in this book, such as laundry items, digital media technologies, furniture, cups of tea and more. It also involves flows of things that are fluid, invisible or intangible, some of which likewise we have already noted in the examples discussed above and in Chapter 3, including flows of electricity, gas, water, fresh air and music. Some researchers are also increasingly making a case for accounting for the role of animals in research into everyday life in the home (see Pink Horst et al. 2016). While as we noted above, the material cultures studies approaches to the home have extensively accounted for the materiality of our homes and how this is manifested through digital technologies, our approach here advances in a different direction. We are concerned with how the home can be conceptualized as an environment made up of the flows of tangible and intangible, invisible things, rather than with putting material culture objects at the centre of the analysis. As we have argued in Chapter 3, the home is an ongoing changing ecology of things and processes. In this chapter we have viewed this through the movement of humans. Yet humans encounter in their movement other things and processes in movement. These may all move in different ways and at different velocities.

Much of the time, and particularly in the examples we have discussed so far in this book, things move through the home with people. We have discussed how digital media technologies accompany people as they move through their homes. In Chapter 3 we discussed the status of laundry as part of the materiality of everyday life in the home. Laundry is also mobile though the home, often going from place to place, and, as Pink has discussed elsewhere, these 'laundry lines' can be followed to see how items of laundry assemble in different areas of the home, and with different configurations of other things and processes, and to specific effects (Pink 2012). Similarly Pink and Postill's research with Indonesian students in Melbourne noted above showed how for some students, the movement of laundry items within the home, and the items that would move with the participants as they chose what to wear outside the home depended on their use of digital weather apps. In developing this analysis Pink and Postill (2016) propose that such a focus on laundry can also offer important new insights into the ways that people actively make themselves feel 'at home' in new places (Pink and Postill 2016). That is, the study of people's movement through the world with 'things' helps us to understand how they navigate their relationships to everyday environments. The movement of things in homes can also form part of the anticipatory modes through which people live in their homes, which we discussed in Chapter 3. For example Figure 4.5 shows how family members leave objects at particular places in the home in order to remind them that these objects need to accompany them somewhere later.

Other flows through the home accompany or encounter with humans in other ways. For example, the flow of sunlight through a window might be something someone seeks out, to follow due to the way it illuminates the pages of a book they are reading, to spend time basking in its warmth, or to use it to dry the laundry. In contrast in UK homes, in the LEEDR project, we found that the flows of cold draughts through gaps in doors, windows, from badly insulated walls, floors or roofs, are encountered with different sentiments and materials. These draughts of cold air in homes also impacted on which rooms might be used at different times of the year in some cases. The movement of water through the home offers an example that helps us to understand how the ways in which people are able to move through homes are also contingent on social relationships, wider systems and infrastructures. For example in one of the LEEDR households, one of the participants described to us how her showering routines were governed both by the family needs in the morning, and by her work and her preference to shower after being at work. In *Laundry*

FIGURE 4.5 *This photograph was taken during a LEEDR research encounter, to note how items were placed at strategic points of the house, in this case as an aide-memoir; the Nintendo DS (dual-screen) games consoles belonged to the family's two girls and were to be taken to piano practice the next day. Piano music and school book bags were added later, along with shopping bags and baskets (as the mother was due to go shopping while the girls were in school).* © LEEDR.

Lives, participants note that at certain times of the day they are able to access stronger water flows than others due to demand, particularly in the morning. As one of the participants points out, if she cannot do her laundry early in the morning, then this impacts on the time she has for her professional work later in the day. Thus we can begin to see, through the example of water that by tracking human movement through the home, and investigating how it is impinged on or facilitated by the movement of other things or resources, we can gain a deeper understanding of how specific configurations of things and processes and the possibilities they bring about are contingent.

Summing up

In this chapter we have outlined how the home might be conceptualized ethnographically through the concept of movement, and we have considered the implications this has for design research and practice.

We have proposed the concept of movement as a means through which to think outside of both conventional discipline-specific paradigms in the social sciences and the conventional categories through which design for/in homes is pursued. While an understanding that movement would be important underpinned the research methods that we used in order to understand how people lived in the home, in our own work we did not set out to centre the findings of our work on movement as an analytical category. Rather, as for other researchers whose work we have discussed in this chapter who have found that movement is integral to the way we need to understand what people *do* in their homes, across other interdisciplinary fields, the significance of movement to everyday life in the home emerged from our engagements with participants and with the research materials we produced with them. In making this point we are not necessarily arguing that movement is *the* concept that should be used to understand human activity in the home. Rather we are demonstrating that in the context of our own work and that of others, it has emerged, along with an understanding of the temporality and environments of homes, as being key to understanding how everyday life in homes proceeds in the past, present and into the future. As such, it offers opportunities for imagining changes, progressions or interruptions to movement as they might play out in future contexts. It allows designers to suspend what are already artificial and sometimes decontextualizing categories of behaviour or practices to interrogate activities as they play out and intersect. Future research might thus follow people and things as they move, perhaps focusing on how movement might happen, restrict or facilitate interrelations as part of and between different processes and sequences of activity. Such an approach also accommodates a future facing element, involving imagining how new forms and sequences of movement might come about and develop, all the while bearing in mind the adaptable and improvisory capacities of people as they live out their lives at home.

That said, as we have emphasized throughout this book, ethnographic findings are produced through an ongoing dialogue between empirical research and theoretical debate. Such dialogues always moreover emerge in ways that are contextual, and this means that in other projects it is possible that other concepts emerge as equally important and might similarly be used as categories for ethnography and design.

5

Methods for researching homes

In the previous chapters we have discussed a series of frames through which we might research, understand and design for homes. Our understandings have been based on in-depth research with participants in their homes, developed through research methods developed across a range of projects, which are always fine-tuned, honed and redesigned for new projects. Methods, as emphasized elsewhere (Pink and Leder Mackley 2012), are not made to be taken 'off the peg', and employed as they are. Therefore, in this chapter, we do not describe set templates for methods that can be used over again. Rather we present a series of design and ethnography research methods that have been engaged to research the home both in our own projects and in those of other researchers, describing the ways that they are effective and the types of knowledge and ways of knowing they can generate. These range between conventional interviewing methods, researcher and participant collaborations, video ethnography methods, self-reporting methods such as diaries, cultural probe methods and self-video recording. The discussion of methods will reflect back on the themes developed in the earlier chapters to discuss the use of these methods in the context of research and intervention related to the *temporalities, environments* and *activities and movement* of home.

Researching everyday life

One of the core issues related to researching and designing for homes and for the people who inhabit them is that the home is a site of everyday life.

This means that it shares all of the challenges and opportunities that are associated with everyday life research, as well as those that are specific to how life plays out in homes. In this section we briefly provide context for the methods discussed below through a discussion of the nature of everyday life as a research site and then in the next section focus in more closely on the home.

Everyday life is not difficult to encounter, it happens ongoingly around us, in an unstoppable flow of events and processes and things of different affordances and properties, which continually configure and reconfigure along the way. This is one of the aspects of everyday life that make it most fascinating, while also being one of its characteristics that has most confounded researchers in seeking to define, 'capture' or document it. This has in the past proved a perennial problem for cultural studies researchers who have grappled with the problematic of disrupting the flow of everyday life in order to document or research it (see Pink 2012 for a discussion of this), for sociologists who have tended to divide everyday life into practices as a manageable research unit (e.g. Shove et al. 2007) or for non-representational scholars who have sought a number of ways in which to co-immerse scholarship and the everyday beyond conventional academic formats such as narrative first-person experience writing. These questions are also relevant for ethnographic and design disciplines; however, in the case of the approach we have advocated in this book, the bringing together of ethnographic and design approaches with a future orientation towards change and intervention, a new perspective comes to the fore. This agenda is already at the core of this book in the three themes that we have pursued – that is temporality, environment and activity. Each of these themes has at its core a concept of movement, in the form of movement through time, the idea that environments are constituted through the continual movement of the things and processes that constitute and reconstitute their ongoingly changing configurations, and the notion of human activity encompassing the ongoing movement of people, and the things that assemble with them, through temporalities and places.

The implication of this understanding that the everyday is part of a world in movement is that we need to engage research and design methods that equally account for this. That is, methods that account for how our participants move, and that move with our participants and the things and processes that they become co-implicated with. The methods outlined below account for this point as they engage with the idea that this process of moving forward in the world is both something that we need to appreciate when researching what people do and how they feel in their homes, and when accounting for how they will move on into their futures *with* design interventions or processes.

Researching in homes

Researchers working in the home have long since recognized that this is a rather special research site. It is a site of incredible interest for several reasons: because it is precisely where people live out the mundane, unremarkable (Tolmie et al. 2002), usually hidden and fundamentally important element of their everyday lives – a site that is ongoingly changing, in the form of the home as 'project' (Pink 2004) as humans modify it and make it as they go along, and also as a site of material change, decay or growth over time; the home is also a site where the ubiquity of media in everyday life has long since been studied. All of these and other research and design interests and areas that intersect with the home make research encounters in the home frequent. As a research site, however, other people's homes are often uncertain places. This indeed is the case not only for researchers but for others who need to go to work in other people's homes – like social workers (Ferguson 2009, 2010), domestic workers (Law 2001; Pratt 1999; Smith 2011), community nurses and other health workers and logistics delivery workers (Pink et al. 2015). This means that doing design ethnographies in homes carries with it a series of issues and possibilities that are particular to the type of research site it presents us with.

The home is an intimate context, it is private and it is where private conversations and activities are played out (Miller 2001; Pink 2004). Being in someone's home with them in a research relationship or conversation can take on something of this intimacy – that is, the atmosphere of home can help to generate a sense of intimacy, confidentiality and trust. In this sense it provides a powerful way in which to engage with otherwise hidden aspects of life in a place which continues to be private. Indeed as researchers, when we work with people in their homes, we need to build strong and genuine networks of trust with them. As researchers we are also responsible for creating a connection between the private worlds we encounter and the lives participants in research experience in them, and public domains of academic and more accessible or popular publications (like the websites and videos associated with this book). This raises ethical issues, and also issues around collaboration and participation, whereby we argue that it is beneficial to go beyond a research relationship with participants that is simply transactional. That is, good design ethnography research involves more than simply going into someone's home, doing research with them there, taking away video or audio recordings, notes or photos and then using these for an analysis and publication. Instead we call for a more deeply moral and ongoing relationship with research participants, whereby when possible, they are given the choice of seeing images or text about themselves if they wish before it is made public and to have a power of veto over the images of them that are ultimately released into a public domain. This ethical process was developed in the LEEDR project and also used by Pink and Astari in the making of the *Laundry Lives* film. LEEDR participants approved all of the video clips of them that were put online in the Energy and Digital Living website, and the *Laundry Lives* key participants viewed the film and approved it before its first public screening. We do not develop an extensive specific discussion of visual research ethics in relation to the home in this book, since there are many adequate discussions of visual ethics elsewhere (see Pink 2013 for a summary, and see http://vrc.org.au/guidelines-for-ethical-visual-research-methods for a useful guide to visual research ethics). However, we do note that using visual research methods in the home is a good example of how research often crosses the boundaries that people usually construct and respect between the public and private in everyday life. Therefore it becomes essential that researchers should seek to acknowledge and navigate this throughout the whole process of research, insight generation, any sharing and publication of visual materials.

Another factor to keep in mind when doing research in other people's homes refers to researcher safety. Again these considerations apply to anyone who works in homes. We may know little about the social, material or technological environments of homes before we enter into them as researchers. While formal researcher safety protocols have not tended to be part of traditional anthropological ethnography in the past, for a number of practical reasons, as well as because the trust through which the ethical relationships discussed above tend to be forged has often also been associated with the well-being of the researcher. However, such systems have developed in other research contexts, and for a good number of institutional as well as practical and sensible reasons safety protocols can play an important and useful role in ethnographic research process, often in the form of formalized processes of checking up on researcher whereabouts and checking in before and after research encounters. Across our projects we have developed various protocols to deal with this. For instance in Sarah Pink's collaborative research with Jennie Morgan and Andrew Dainty, Jennie spent some time accompanying community health workers and logistics workers on home visits and deliveries. While this research mainly showed up the ways in which these workers dealt with their own safety in such situations, as described elsewhere, it was also illustrative relating to the ways that Jennie needed to navigate the fact that she was doing (field)work in those same homes (Pink et al. 2015). In that example the researcher was already accompanied because she was doing research with the workers rather than the householders. In earlier work, in ways typical of anthropological ethnographic fieldwork it simply did not occur to the researcher that she needed to take any particular precautions, other than ensuring that someone usually knew she had gone to do such fieldwork (see for example Pink 2004). However, now that researcher safety issues are increasingly recognized, it is correspondingly more common for ethnographers to visit homes in pairs or to have a safety procedure in place. For instance during the video ethnography research that led to *Laundry Lives* (Pink and Astari 2015), an anthropologist and filmmaker visited homes in Indonesia together. For the LEEDR project home visits, researchers always visited in pairs during the first stage of visits (the Getting to Know You visits discussed below) and for the subsequent video ethnography visits either made in pairs or used a structured safety protocol. In this project a researcher safety protocol was useful as a safety feature at the beginning of the project when the participants and researchers were unknown to each other. However as we learned, such protocols should also be flexible so that they can be reshaped over time in relation to changing fieldwork relationships, and as collaborative arrangements and friendships between participants and ethnographers emerge.

When doing interdisciplinary research we also need to consider how the home might be considered and experienced as a different kind of research site for researchers from different disciplines. We have found, that in our own experiences of collaboration, social scientists and design researchers have had similar sensitivities in relating to the home as a lived environment. In contrast, designers working in our team have found that researchers working in more technical disciplines are more likely to view it as a lab. For example, design researchers have found themselves in situations of needing to champion the aesthetic dimensions of items of research equipment that researchers from technical disciplines need to install in homes. However there are also different approaches to researching in homes within design research. For example in some fields of design (and in anthropology) there are concerns about giving participants things to do that disrupt normal everyday life, such as the use of extensive diary studies alongside technical studies. In some design traditions, which stand outside the co-design approach that we advocate in this book, researchers seek to study people in the home as discretely as possible (e.g. the HCI researchers Crabtree and Rodden (2004b) describe the discrete installation of video cameras within sixteen family homes in order to understand the routines of home but not disrupt the 'business of everyday life'). In contrast, forms of participation and reflection are core to the methods we outline here. This is a key common ground between third paradigm approaches within HCI research (Harrison et al. 2007; Pink et al. 2013) and the sensory ethnography approach developed by Pink (2015), both of which take a broadly phenomenological perspective.

During our discussions of methods in the following sections, wherever relevant, we highlight these overlaps as well as contrasts between design and ethnographic methods. Indeed when undertaking interdisciplinary work, it is important to create correspondences between different approaches but not to assume that superficial similarities necessarily mean similar conceptualizations or commitments. We do not generalize about differences here, since they often emerge in the *doing* of research and analysis, given that as we have noted methods evolve and emerge on a project-by-project basis. However, a recent research experiment highlights how and where superficial similarities and possible differences between ethnographic anthropology and design research processes can emerge. Sarah Pink, Yoko Akama and participants found through a two-day co-exploration of ideas of and experiences of uncertainty between ethnographers, designers and artists in Melbourne, Australia, in 2014, that it was possible to define the different ways that uncertainty is located in the practice of ethnographers and designers and how different ways of approaching and knowing about the world can both come up against each other, and conversely sometimes be felt to be coherent. In such messy research and intervention contexts, it was argued that a core methodological aim might be to seek to embrace uncertainty in ways that encompass the needs and interests of both ethnographers and designers, as a mode through which to work together (Pink et al. 2015). Disciplinary differences will always emerge in new forms in ways that are project specific. In Chapter 1 we have discussed some of the more systematic analyses of this, which compare disciplines. The *Un/Certainty* iBook (Pink, Akama and participants 2015) discusses this in relation to the commentaries of researchers and designers, through statements, video clips and analysis, and offers readers a means through which to reflect on how such issues might arise and be treated in specific projects.

Using short-term and intensive ethnographic and design research methods

The research methods that we discuss here have in common that they are all based on relatively short-term encounters with research participants, which might happen only once or twice. In some cases these have been part of a longer-term research process in which participants have been involved in a series of different activities over a period of four years. In other cases they have been developed within considerably shorter-term projects, but in which researchers have still stayed in contact with participants over a period of time after the initial research encounter itself. However, there are other reasons why short-term ethnographic methods are needed, for instance in order to fit with the timescales of applied research agendas and the deadlines of the organizations and other stakeholders that we might collaborate or partner with.

Research undertaken in other people's homes tends to be short term for various reasons: it is difficult to spend extended periods of time in homes – unless living there as a house guest, which constitutes a rather different research relationship that is quite typical of long-term anthropological research.

However even if one was to live as a house guest for a period of several months, while doing research about or in homes, it would be impossible to undertake research in more than very few homes during even a long period of fieldwork of 12 months. Where project timescales are much shorter, this would be impossible.

The methods we discuss were also played out in different types of relationship with households. Sometimes they have involved working with the same set of households, using several different methods over a four-year period, or a smaller set of methods during this period. In other cases only one or two of the methods have been used, and the amount of contact we have been able to have with participants during the whole research process has been limited to one or two meetings. The methods discussed are generically speaking participatory methods, but some include researcher-led videos, researcher-led creative activities and then more participant-led activities, such as a range of self-reporting methods.

Using interview methods in homes

Conventional interviewing methods have long since been the mainstay of qualitative research in the social sciences and humanities. There is a wide literature on this topic, which provides a good source of advice and reflection on the types of interviews that might be undertaken, their theoretical underpinnings and practical methods (Seale 1998; Skinner 2012; Oakley 2000; Rapley 2004; Sherman Heyl 2001; O'Reilly 2005; Pink 2015). Although interviews are limited in terms of the types of embodied, sensory and atmospheric experiences, memories, imaginaries and aspirations that they might reveal or imply when compared with other more embodied and performative methods (see below), they do offer focused ways in which to gain verbal accounts, narratives and reflexive understandings of participants' everyday lives and worlds. Much of everyday communication is verbal and thus many of the ways in which such aspects of life might be communicated in a research encounter are likewise verbal.

However, we situate a design ethnography approach to interviewing differently to these more conventional renderings of the interview. In the approach developed here, the interview has some of the characteristics associated with conventional interviews, such as its intimacy and its development as a kind of 'conversation' (Oakley 2000), potentially a source of practical information as well as of representation, or as a (specific) way of participating in other people's worlds (Pink 2015). In contrast, in many existing discussions of the interview it is seen as a method to be used in isolation (with the exception of the ethnographic interview (Sherman Heyl 2001; O'Reilly 2005)), whereby interviewing becomes the method used, rather than part of a suite of methods or an element of a more complex method. As is evident in the context of the methods discussed below, some of which involved physical activities, making things or video recording, in our own work, verbal interviews have become either more than just interviews, or they have been strands that are interwoven through embodied and performative methods and research encounters.

Whether or not situated within these more complex activities, there is, however, a certain specificity associated with doing interviews in homes, which can impact on the interview and on the research encounter and what we learn from it in a number of ways. As we have noted, the home is a private place, and it is a site where participants tend to have all their 'things' around them. It is also a place where they consume and produce, food, drinks, possibly other things, and that they ongoingly renew through everyday processes like cleaning and laundry. When entering someone else's home, it is important to keep in mind that this is the very world that we are entering and starting to share with a participant. Even if simply undertaking an interview in a home, we are already, once through the door, experiencing the same floor surfaces underfoot and breathing the same air as the research participant – that is, we are *in* their environment, and inhaling and feeling it as we move through it. This means that we enter into sensory environments, the significance of which is important to attend to. Elsewhere, Pink has outlined how these considerations can help us reflect on the home as a site for learning through one-to-one interviews:

> By sitting with another person in their living room, in *their* chair, drinking *their* coffee from one of *their* mugs, or when drinking together in a café, one begins in some small way to occupy the world in a way that is similar to them. As the interview progresses, images, sounds, artefacts and emotions might be shared and other people may come and go. The interview and its environment create a place-event, where researcher and interviewee are mutually emplaced as they move along its narrative. They are in a situation where they interact in ways often more intense than in everyday life, producing heightened reflections and new ways of knowing. Interviews are not only places where researchers learn about other people's experiences, but where interviewees might arrive at new levels of awareness about their own lives and experiences. (Pink 2015: 80)

Interviewing in the home indeed involves entering into the mundane, intimate and private sphere of participants' lives. It can be a research encounter that goes beyond being verbal. Indeed this is one of the reasons why it becomes useful to connect such more formal verbal interviewing methods with other ways of knowing and learning about people's lives. For instance, when researching uses of mobile digital technologies in homes through interviews, the technologies might become part of the interviews, used, to show the activities that are being spoken about. This, in some cases, has included participants demonstrating how they might use their tablets or other devices as part of the interview as a way of showing what they do at home (see Pink Sinanan et al. 2016). For instance as part of the interviews that she undertook within the Locating the Mobile research project in Australia in 2015, Pink asked participants about their mobile phone use biographies. The biographies of mundane things, including those of technologies, are often bound up with those of people. This means that when interviewing people in their homes, they often bring material objects into the interview and/or draw from those things that are encountered. Mobile phone biographies, Pink found, in some cases, were kept materially in the home, in the form of the mobile phones themselves. Participants went and sought out their old phones and told the story of their use through them, while being video recorded. For instance, one participant, Ben recalled his prior phone history, before talking about the several current phones he laid out in front of us on the table:

> So this has been a great phone except for one thing, the GPS is absolutely rubbish. But this other one works so I use that when I need accurate measurements when I go for a run. This I'm sending for recycling. These other two are dead, I'm just slow to throw things away. But I used two phones when I was away. I kept an Irish sim and a UK sim. I think I kept them all because you needed an extra one when you went to another country. Phones are really annoying to unlock here. They are locked to networks and I don't think they do that in other countries now. I went to Malaysia and Indonesia and I tried to get one unlocked and they were like what do mean locked?

Indeed, in this way sometimes interviews can become blurred with the home tour as in the following example from the LEEDR project, shown in Figure 5.1.

Some everyday life biographies, experiences and activities that are stored or enacted in homes are often best encountered in this way, by extending the interview to include things and activities, rather than just words.

Not all interviews are with single participants, and in the context of doing research in households, it is important to seek to engage some participation of the wider household as a group, even if not all household members are able to continue to engage in the research process throughout the whole project. An example of this was developed in the LEEDR project by the design team, in the form of the 'Getting to Know You' (known as GTKY interviews) stage of the

FIGURE 5.1 *The encounter with this participant started as more of an interview over coffee, then the participant began to show Kerstin around the house, taking the coffee with her. Here she was showing Kerstin her kitchen book shelf, which we learned was part of what makes the home feel right for her, and she explained she couldn't find anywhere else for her books than this space in the kitchen.* © LEEDR.

FIGURE 5.2 *The GTKY shared meal interviews.* © LEEDR.

research. This was the first research encounter that the ethnographic and design teams had with each household, and served not simply as an interview but also as an introduction, and created a context where a series of other collective research activities was also undertaken. This enabled the research team to build a detailed picture of participant lifestyles, energy awareness, future aspirations, and habitual occupation patterns in a very limited timeframe while making the process a pleasant one for the participants. Although it was a design-led research activity, whenever possible a member of the ethnography team also attended and participated, meaning that she was also able to secure an introduction to the household in preparation for the more one-to-one research activities that she would undertake. The GTKY interview took place over a take-away meal paid for by the project but chosen by the family. A shared meal around the dining room or kitchen table provides a familiar context for inviting others into the home and for the participants to engage with the researchers. Kanstrup (2006) similarly describes how early visits to participants' homes were confined to the dining table as trust was established between researchers and participants. The LEEDR team was particularly keen to establish this trust before the video tours where participants would be asked to introduce more private areas of their homes such as bedrooms and bathrooms to the visiting researchers. The shared meal also provided the context for involving all family members in the interview with creative activities after the food used to engage and involve children as young as five (see Mitchell et al. 2014). The time together, with the families permission, was voice-recorded using a small Dictaphone. This allowed conversation to flow naturally among family members and researchers, providing an opportunity to begin to understand the interplay between family members.

Touring the home with participants

Video tours, or audio tours sometimes incorporating photography, are increasingly used for researching everyday life in the home, and have figured considerably in the projects we have discussed in the preceding chapters of this book. There are various ways to conceptualize recorded tours. For instance, often they are considered as 'mobile recorded interviews', which allow researchers and participants to utilize 'domestic spaces and materials as prompts to frame conversations about what happens, where and why' (Hinton et al. 2012: 4). Especially in the context of HCI research and the exploration of technologies in the home, video tours have served to explore the situated contexts of devices and interactions, and to more generally document the research context and environment. Observation and documentation are also at the heart of recent uses of CCTV cameras in the home, where the idea is to record everyday activities as and when they happen (Martens and Scott 2004; Martens 2012).

In our own research (see for instance Pink 2013, 2015), we have departed from this emphasis on observation and documentation in order to advance these methods through a particular approach that involves using the video tour as a collaborative research tool, and a form of place-making (Pink 2007). Following this approach, video is used to help us to engage with participants as they show us around the home and explore together how everyday life plays out in moments when we are not there to observe. This involves going beyond research practices that use video as a tool to 'record' or 'document' everyday life, as if such activity and experience could be actually caught on camera in its entirety or was transparent in meaning (cf. Sunderland and Denny 2007). Instead, following our approach, we consider video to be a route through people's homes that can allow us to imagine everyday life as it had already happened, and how it could unfold for our participant households or individuals in different situations and contexts. In participatory design research, likewise, the idea of taking video beyond 'hard' data has been important. For instance, Buur et al. (2000: 21) consider the designer's working cycle through video as one of 'recording-editing-viewing'. As such they suggest that 'video recordings from e.g. a contextual inquiry are no longer hard data but rather the first attempts to create stories that frame the design problem and impose order on the complexity of everyday life' (2000: 21).

In our own experience we have found that video tours gave participants the chance to tell us about, demonstrate performatively for us, or show us evidence of examples of things that had or could happen in the home, and of how things 'usually' were. It also enabled us to use the home itself as a material and sensory probe through which to ask questions, invite participants to evoke experiences and to learn about how it was to live in that particular environment. The use of the video tour is also congruent with the emphasis on temporality, movement and environment that we advance in this book, since it enables researchers to explore each of these dimensions of everyday life with participants in their homes.

Simultaneously video recordings can provide a lasting slice of research experience for researchers, of being with participants in their homes, following them around and, in doing so, sensing our way through their homes. Consumer anthropologists have advocated video as allowing viewers to experience some of the 'sociocultural texture' (Sunderland and Denny 2007: 270) of people's everyday lives, thus enabling learning through a 'form of "acquaintance"' (MacDougall, 1997: 286). As we have written elsewhere (Leder Mackley and Pink 2013), this experiential dimension of video was important to our work and, combined with our individual experiences of conducting video tours with participants, it meant that – to some degree – we could also delve into each other's video work as though we had been there when the video was being generated. This is both a combination of having fulfilled the role of video ethnographer and, thus, a familiarity with the experience of the tour as research encounter, as it is about developing forms of empathy for the positioning of fellow researchers as they undertake video ethnography.

The home video tour like other methods does not involve pre-established series of stages, but is rather adapted according to the research question, the particular participant(s), and their home. It should always be undertaken with respect for the privacy of the participant and as a collaborative exercise, whereby the participant is invited to show their home to the extent that they feel comfortable and necessary to undertake the shared exploration they are sharing with the researcher. In past projects different themes have featured. Therefore whereas in her earlier projects on the home Pink invited participants to tell her how they cared for each room and how they had adapted it over time (Pink 2004), or about the laundry items in their rooms (Pink 2012), in the LEEDR project participants were asked to tell us what they did in each room to make the room 'feel right'. Here the intention was to learn with them about how this process created demand for energy. Such activities enable us to learn with participants. They do not show us the everyday reality of domestic tasks as they are played out, but instead they enable participants to reflect on and create abstractions or aggregates of their experiences of undertaking these tasks over longer periods of time than those we would be able to actually observe as researchers. These rich and collaboratively produced understandings offer different types of knowledge to those presented from

FIGURE 5.3 *In this daytime video tour the woman participant who led it focused our attention towards how the family would come together in the different rooms she showed us, as well as the domestic technologies that were part of the home. She took the tour through the children's shared bedroom (where there was a seemingly passed down TV), moving through the living/dining room, to show the computer desk in the dining room and point out the washing machine socket.* © LEEDR.

outside observation studies, and we argue that they enable significant insights into participant perspectives and experience.

As with all video materials produced during LEEDR, our ethics procedure determined that participants were able to review videos before we shared them with the rest of the team and edit any content they did not feel comfortable with. A follow-up visit allowed participants to further comment and, in cases where only one family member had shown us around the house (often one of the adults), it also invited reflections from other family members. These visits were further revealing in that they demonstrated any changes that had happened in the home in the weeks and sometimes months between our visits;

FIGURE 5.4 *Different family members led this tour and also participated as their everyday life activities continued as we went through the home. The tour happened close to Christmas 2011, so the mother of the family contributed while decorating the Christmas cake, and the father described how furniture would be moved according to times of year and special occasions. One of the children showed Kerstin around the top of the house, including their parents' bedroom and the bathroom, the colours of which he had chosen (although the bathroom was completely redecorated towards the end of our research). One of the moveable objects in the home was the 'family computer', which was at the time on the kitchen table, making the kitchen into a workspace, and laundry was a key part of the materiality of the home (see Chapter 3). © LEEDR.*

these could include the acquisition, disposal or changed ownership of domestic technologies, the use of rooms according to season or the arrival/departure of guests and relatives, changes in family pets and so on. Reviewing the video tours brought into focus changes that would have otherwise gone almost unnoticed in the general busyness and 'ongoingness' of everyday family life.

While we have advocated for the virtues of video in understanding people in their homes, and expounded in particular their value and use for understanding the embodied, and unspoken ways of knowing that participants have about their everyday environments, video is not the only, and not always the most appropriate, method for use when exploring homes with people. Methods should be designed to suit research questions and contexts, and the use of video may not always be suitable for particular groups of participant or for the research question being explored (Pink 2013). In some cases moreover in projects that generally use video, and where the particular sample of participants supersedes the need to follow exactly the same method with each participant, photography and audio can be substituted with those participants who do not wish to be video recorded. While some research approaches would insist that the same research procedure is followed identically with each participant, in ethnographic work this is not necessarily considered important. This is because we know that each research counter is created through the development of a specific relationship between the researcher and the participant. Often it is reflexivity about this relationship and the specific circumstances through which knowledge was produced that matters more than the meticulous repetition of exactly the same procedure with each participant.

Video re-enactments

As the examples we have discussed throughout this book have shown, the home is a site of, among other things, the everyday unspoken and embodied ways of knowing, which are part of how people do those 'background' tasks like laundry and switching off and on appliances at bedtime. However such 'invisible' aspects of the everyday are often not even immediately apparent to the ethnographer, but rather they need to be collaboratively unravelled and revealed through the encounters that we create between researchers and participants. Traditional anthropological ethnographers might have investigated such things through repeated observation, however, as we have noted, doing this in homes is often not viable, and interviews do not tell the full story of the embodied, sensory in situ experience of undertaking everyday tasks and routines.

The kinds of things that we are often interested in asking participants to share with us when we do research about homes and lives that are part of them are frequently surprising to participants. Across our various projects participants have looked at us with curiosity, often we have wondered if they think we must be crazy to be interested in, for instance, what they do on the way to bed at night, or how they wash their dishes, load their washing machines or hang out their laundry to dry. A memorable example of this is shown in video 23 on the Energy and Digital Living website (see Figure 5.5). In this video, Alan, one of our participants, was showing Sarah and Kerstin his bedtime routine, which Sarah filmed while Kerstin accompanied. The re-enactment involved Alan taking us on what would be his usual route to bed at night. Because he worked nights and all his family would already be asleep when he arrived home, he started the tour at the moment he stepped

FIGURE 5.5 *Alan's video re-enactment of his bedtime routine in Energy and Digital Living: video 23 at www.energyanddigitalliving.com.* © LEEDR.

through the door. This was in fact his garage door as he would park his car outside his garage and then open the electrical garage door to walk through the garage where things were stored, into his backyard and then through to the conservatory. The routine he showed us was a unique example of the previously invisible, unwitnessed nightly route through his home, the kind of thing he would not usually be asked to describe, and something his sleeping family would not witness either. For instance when we were halfway through, Alan stopped at the bottom of the stairs unsure if we wanted him to continue until Sarah reassured him that we did. Later at the end of the video clip, Sarah asked Alan if there was a reason why he went through the house as he did – she imagined it might be so that he would not wake up his family, or perhaps to save electricity given that he did not switch the lights on in every room that he went through. However, as Alan made clear, these were not really things he thought about since it was 'about putting on the lights I need'. Such everyday activities are not necessarily strategically planned in order to achieve particular domestic goals, but rather they are contingent – doing what you need to do, in order to be able to then do what comes next; that is, they are part of the ongoingness of everyday life as it is lived out.

While video re-enactments are sometimes unusual, novel, fun or interesting for participants, they are also a serious and theoretically informed research method which seeks to engage researchers and participants together in exploring ways of knowing about their activities in and experiences of the environments they live in. The re-enactment approach seeks to focus on two ways of knowing about homes. First, on what participants can easily articulate verbally about particular activities and environments, which they might be prompted to discuss or reminded of when they are actually in those environments, examining them and reflecting on what they do there with the researcher. Second, on those ways of knowing that are embodied and sensory, not necessarily ever articulated in spoken words, and not the kinds of things that participants would even think of discussing. This includes, for instance, bedtime routines and routes through the home, such as that of Alan mentioned above (and see Pink and Leder Mackley 2014), as well as washing up (Pink 2012), bathroom cleaning (Pink 2011), doing the laundry (Pink 2005; Pink, Leder Mackley and Moroşanu 2015) and mobile and social media use in the home (Pink, Sinanan et al. 2016). The theory and practice of re-enactment methods are discussed at length elsewhere (Pink and Leder Mackley 2014), and we recommend readers who are interested in a deeper and longer analytical discussion to that article. Here we take a more home-focused and practical approach to introduce the key ways in which re-enactments may be beneficially conceptualized, planned, carried out, and what they might mean analytically in terms of the types of knowing that they are able to generate and/or make accessible.

A re-enactment is conceptualized, in the context of research methodology, as a collaborative and reflexive activity developed between researcher and participant. It is important not to confuse this with an observation of actual everyday events as they are 'always' played out. Placing this in the context of our discussion of the home, several of the points that we have already made in earlier chapters frame this: first, we have emphasized that the home is a continually shifting site, and people, things and technologies move through it; second, we have shown how people ongoingly improvise in their everyday lives in their homes, therefore we would not expect the same routine to be enacted in exactly the same way every time.

Connecting with the three thematic chapters of this book – which have focused on temporalities, environments and activity and movement – re-enactments also have specific relevance to research that engages with each of these three elements, and indeed attends to the relationships between them. For instance, in relation to temporalities of home, re-enactments can focus on transition moments or processes of renewal in the home. These are frequently mundane moments related to cleaning or refreshing objects or environments, or shifts between daytime and night-time, coming home or going out. There are indeed many of these in everyday life, and we suggest that this approach is particularly useful for understanding how they play out. Because these re-enactments focus on the routines of everyday life, they attend to the way in which everyday life is ongoing, marked by particular regular events. However re-enactments also connect to the theme of the temporalities of home in the ways in which they enable participants to bring together abstract and cumulative versions of their everyday routines. As noted above, a re-enactment is not a single observed authentic instance of the routine taking place, but rather it is a pulling together of biographically or historically accrued ways of knowing about that routine or task, to produce a performance of it that is both particular and abstract at the same time. By this we mean that the performance of the re-enactment is of course specific – a one-off event – but that it is abstract in that it draws on and seeks to stand for the many times this has been performed before.

With reference to the environments of home, the re-enactment methodology engages with the physical material, sensory and digital elements of the environment of home in a number of ways. First, it helps us to understand, as researchers and in collaboration with participants, how the environments of home are made and remade as people move through them. They provide a narrative through which to explore how participants engage with these environments of home, how they experience them and which elements come to the fore for them. The very environments in which we ask participants to undertake the re-enactments, however, are also important as probes and prompts in the research process. Here we suggest that it is because we ask participants to undertake re-enactments in situ – that is, in the very places where they usually enact the same processes or routines – the material and sensory elements of their homes help them to recall, and to perform their embodied ways of knowing, and to verbally articulate their reflections.

In relation to movement and activity, re-enactments are usually of an activity, and such activities tend to involve moving through the home, moving on in time and moving from one state towards another. The re-enactment method has been used, as noted above, across different types of activity. Some such activities involve moving *through the home*, such as bedtime routines, going out routines and arriving home routines. Laundry routines and other actual domestic tasks also involve moving through the home although in slightly different ways, since they engage movement as part of the accomplishment of a task where the focus is on material and sensory transformation of actual objects, rather than on the process of arriving in one part of the home from another.

Finally, it is important to understand re-enactments in relation to the types of knowledge or ways of knowing that they make available to researchers. As argued elsewhere (Pink and Leder Mackley 2014), the re-enactment brings to the fore tacit, normally unspoken, knowledge, which can be understood in a number of ways, and which might work at different levels of consciousness and intentionality. First, as embodied memory, a kind of 'muscle memory' which comes to the fore as the body is engaged in physical activity. This could be seen for instance in the ways in which people move around in their homes in ways that are known, but not spoken of, when someone reaches for a light switch on the wall without needing to look, knows that the door has been locked because they have felt it click, and when to adjust her or his step when arriving at the top or bottom of the staircase. Second, re-enactments can demonstrate performative ways of showing not only what is done, but also some of the affective elements of what is done, such as performing tasks in ways that intentionally resist conventions. This might include ways of cleaning the home that purposefully evade perceived standards or conventions of housewifely practice, as in examples given in Pink's earlier work about gendered ways of looking after homes (Pink 2004), whereby for some participants there were certain areas of the bathroom they would not clean, or differentiating frequencies with which they would clean their homes. Third, re-enactments, as played out in our work, also invite participants to develop new levels of self-reflection about these activities, in that as they perform and comment on them, there are certain aspects of the activity that they are able to articulate verbally, in the form of explanations, rationales or other sometimes surprising revelations.

Examples of re-enactments can be seen in videos 23, 28, 29, 31 and 32 at www.energyanddigitalliving.com.

In-practice studies of everyday human activity

In-practice studies of everyday human activity bear some similarities to the re-enactment methods we have discussed above, in that they do involve participants performing normal everyday routines with researchers video recording or documenting in other ways. Therefore they are re-enactments but of a different kind (see Pink and Leder Mackley 2014). The key difference is that while there may be some shifts and changes in everyday routines in order to accommodate the researcher's presence, the activities being performed are played out within the context of an actual instance of a functional everyday life routine occurring. For instance, while they would be doing so specifically in the context of participating in a research encounter, and might for example have saved their laundry (Pink and Leder Mackley 2014; Pink and Astari 2015; Pink 2005), bathroom cleaning (Pink 2011) or washing up (e.g. Pink 2012) for that event, they are using the actual materials, technologies and processes to achieve something within an everyday life context. Therefore the showing of the activity at an abstract level as in the re-enactment method is still part of this task; however, the specificity of how it is performed on that particular occasion and the ways that this is navigated are also present in the encounter.

In the context of the LEEDR project, our 'everyday activity' visits (as we introduced them to participants) attended to specific areas of everyday life, first, because they were related to energy consumption and, second, because we considered them as relevant to possible design interventions. We arranged to visit families when we knew they were cooking a regular family meal or when they were due to deal with their laundry, and we usually combined these visits with engaging family members in re-enactments and conversations about their bathroom uses as well as their domestic encounters with digital media. Digital media made energy consumption necessary in their own right but were also integral to our attempts at designing solutions for energy demand reduction. As with other ethnographic methods employed on the project, we allowed our approach to adapt to participants' availability and preferences. We aimed to engage with events as and when they were due to occur naturally within the flow of everyday life. However, some families invited us to spend longer stretches of time with them, enabling us to attend to some of the other details of everyday family life in which these practices were embedded and entangled. Other families arranged for shorter, more activity-focused visits.

Inevitably, there were differences in the researcher's depth and variety of experiences; our video materials, on the other hand, were relatively comparable across energy-related practices, as we generally chose not to

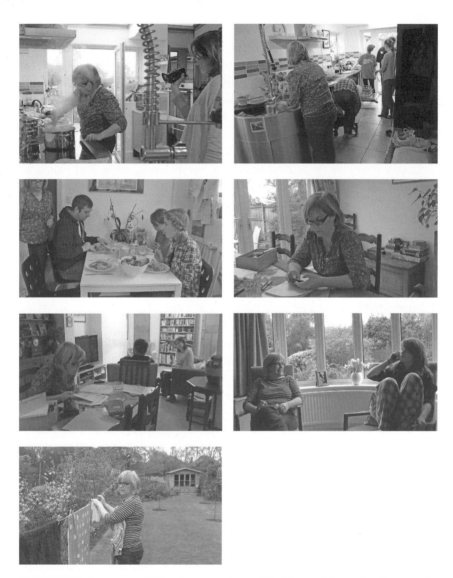

FIGURE 5.6 *Roxana and Kerstin spent time with this participant family over the course of three days. Among other things, they attended a regular Friday evening family meal and some Saturday morning breakfast and laundry chores. Media uses were explored as they formed part of family members' everyday activities, including working from home.* © LEEDR.

record every minute of our visits but those moments that were most closely related to cooking/cleaning, personal hygiene, laundry and digital media activities. This could sometimes be a challenge, bringing to the fore how what are commonly defined as particular everyday practices cannot always be easily delineated and, instead, often overlap with or 'spill' into other areas of life and work at home. One example of this is Vicki's bathroom routine which we also discuss elsewhere (Pink and Leder Mackley 2015, see video 36 at www.energyanddigitalliving.com). Vicki told us that she usually takes a daily bath, in the mornings, although this might vary on the weekend. Rather than getting straight into the bathtub, her routine starts with cleaning the tub, sink and toilet, and hanging up towels that had been left on the floor by others. Once in the bath, Vicki often listens to Radio 4 and reads materials for work. As with other doors in the house, Vicki told us that she preferred for the bathroom door to be open during baths. Hence, depending on the time of the day, she might get interrupted by other members of the family going in and out of the bathroom, as part of their routine of 'getting ready' or just for a chat. Vicki's bathroom routine thus incorporates a range of activities which could be extracted from the research encounter and analysed in isolation; for us it made sense to consider the overall processes and sequences of activity in order to study their interrelations.

Whereas the LEEDR video tours were at times too long and involved for younger participants, the everyday activity work lent itself well to working with families, including younger children. This is because children could actively choose their level of engagement during our visits and, likewise, we could partake in and learn more about their activities as and when they happened. This was especially the case in relation to their already dispersed uses of media technologies around the home.

Again, a challenge was to choose the depth of engagement with media technologies, whether for instance we sought to learn details of how participants navigated websites or video games, or instead needed to know at a higher level how these forms of media engagement were relevant within the context of wider routines and activities in the home. These choices were not always straightforward; in some cases, the way a media device was used was also directly linked to its energy consumption (e.g. mobile devices).

The *Laundry Lives* documentary includes a series of edited video recordings of participants demonstrating how they did their laundry. These recordings were made using a similar methodology, which was employed both in Pink and Postill's research with Indonesians in Melbourne (Pink and Postill 2016) and in the video ethnography undertaken by Astari in Indonesia. This is also an interesting example of how the methodology can be adapted across projects of different lengths, sizes and foci. The documentation of laundry processes

FIGURE 5.7 *Children's media engagements during LEEDR's 'everyday activity' visits.* © *LEEDR.*

here, and in Pink's earlier work (e.g. Pink 2012), was developed through a technique that involved elements of the re-enactment methods discussed above, and elements of the in-practice studies discussed here. Similar methods were used by Pink in the research in homes discussed in her *Home Truths* (2004) and *Situating Everyday Life* (2012), and they tend to be more suited to studies that are focused on particular sets of activities. In contrast, because the LEEDR research was of a longer term and explored a range of entangled everyday life activities, the approach taken to spending time with people in the homes was extended.

Participatory floor plan activity and timeline methods

While the in-practice studies are designed to follow participants as they engage in activity, the floor plan activity focused on participants from a different direction. It can be used in conjunction with in-practice studies, and other methods discussed above, to consider, with participants, how they move around in and engage with activities in their homes. The method, as we used it, was developed with the aim to interactively generate an occupancy flow map of a whole family's routines throughout the home during the hypothetical 'average' weekday and weekend day. Floor plans of the family home were prepared in advance, and the family members were asked to talk through their behaviours on a given day while putting down numbered stickers in sequence. Three sheets were prepared for each day, covering the morning, afternoon and evening periods. Mapping techniques have been used in the past by a number of researchers studying behaviour, and have ranged from technology-based trackers (Aipperspach and Hooker 2005) to 'lo-fi' felt board representations of home (Mateas et al. 1996).

In the context of the example discussed here, this mapping activity was primarily an empathic design tool. Empathic design is a 'research approach that is directed towards building creative understanding of users and their everyday lives for new product development' (Postma et al. 2012). In empathic design, mapping activities are viewed as 'cognitive toolkits' (Sanders and Dandavate 1999) which generate 'stories' which tell us how people understand and misunderstand things, places and events. Of specific interest to this research into technologically mediated behaviour is their ability to reveal 'the intuitive relationships between system components' (ibid.). Our research showed that one of the key advantages of this mapping activity was that it allowed the researchers to delve into the busy lives of the participants and understand the rhythms and constraints that shape them

FIGURE 5.8 *The floor plan activity.* © *LEEDR.*

in a very short timeframe. Beyond the empathic qualities of the method, the mapping activity was considered important for several other reasons; first, it provided triangulation of the verbal responses from the interview; second, it provided a spatial record of occupancy and energy use 'hotspots' which could be used to inform both energy monitoring research carried out by engineers, and possible subsequent design interventions; third, it generated unforeseen responses and dynamics from the family members providing greater insight into the group; and lastly, it highlighted the nature of habitual behaviours.

The final design of the activity consisted of a set of floor plan drawings of the home (one for morning, afternoon and night) for both weekdays and weekends. Each family member was given a set of numbered colour-specific stickers which they could lay down in sequential order as they talked through their 'typical' day. The activity produced a set of 'flow plans' which provided an excellent graphical record of a self-reported weekday and weekend day.

Such participatory methods offer researchers and participant ways to explore and document everyday life together to create shared research and design resources. They often involve the use of materials designed for these documentation purposes and specifically developed and tailored for use in homes, as were the floor plans, which were developed individually for each household. For instance, as part of another project (CALEBRE), the timeline participatory method, a co-design tool was developed to help participants reflect on the home improvements they had made since they moved into their home (Mallaband et al. 2013). Here, a set of magnetic cards were designed to act as prompts depicting life events and possible home improvements. Working together the design researcher and the family used a magnetic whiteboard to create a timeline of their home using the cards as prompts. The result was a rich narrative of the householders' relationship to their home over time around which the researchers were able to explore why they had made the changes they had undertaken and how they went about each project.

Arts-based methods: The Tactile Time collage

While it has been argued that Arts-Based Research (ABR) has its own paradigm (Leavy 2015) different from both qualitative and quantitative paradigms, methodological tools inspired by visual and performing arts are sometimes used as part of qualitative research alongside interviews and other standard methods. For example, methods inspired by the visual arts, such as drawings, can be employed as part of interviews both as an elicitation technique and as a way of accessing and representing different levels of experience related to non-linguistic dimensions (Bagnoli 2009). The use of visual arts-based methods is most often participatory: the people taking part in research create drawings, collages or graphic novels in order to engage with the topic and questions addressed by the research. For example, in her work with young adults on migration and identity, Bagnoli (2009) asked participants to draw a self-portrait adding the people and things they considered important at that moment in life. Through the process of drawing the self-portrait, people were able to engage with, and to represent, in a direct and evocative way, their dilemmas and emotions related to being a migrant.

Collage is a visual arts technique that consists in mixing and juxtaposing pictures and materials, very often making use of newspaper and magazine cuttings. In her work on everyday temporalities and digital media usage, Roxana proposed the Tactile Time collage method as a way of mapping home time and of triggering a discussion over the qualities of time in domestic settings. The method was employed with families during a research encounter taking place in their homes. The participants were provided with a collage kit consisting in: pictures of ordinary digital devices, such as mobile phones, laptops and TV sets, and of food and beverage items; cardboard and coloured felt pens; and a variety of textile fabrics. The family members that wanted to take part in the task – usually between three and four people – were then asked to work collaboratively in creating a collage that showed the way in which they spent time, together and individually, around specific technologies, such as the living room TV set. They wrote down the time when they normally switched the device on and off all around the day, adding pictures of other items they used or consumed on those occasions, such as food and beverage items, books and newspapers, mobile phones and laptops. This part of the encounter was audio-recorded in order to capture the rich discussion that went on between family members while doing the task. During the next stage, they were asked to individually choose a textile material that represented the way time felt for them in each of those moments and to explain their choice. The participants felt the fabrics in pursuit of one, or a combination of, textile materials that would express their subjective and non-linguistic experience of how time felt in a specific situation. In order to capture this process of touching, feeling and thinking, this stage was video recorded.

The Tactile Time collage method was designed specifically for this research and it was one of several participatory methods that were employed, alongside semi-structured interviews and participant observation, as part of long-term ethnographic fieldwork. Therefore, the set of collages was not analysed in isolation, but in relation to the other materials that resulted from the research. The insights that emerged from this research encounter were further explored, particularly, in writing about family time, and in looking at the forms of sociality that people and technologies engendered in domestic settings (Moroşanu

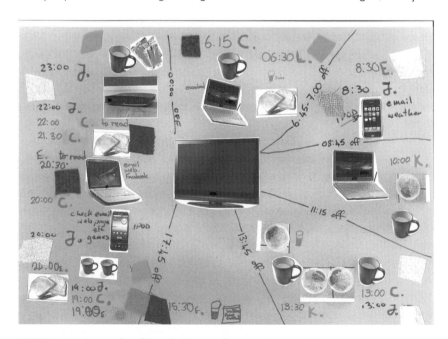

FIGURE 5.9 *Example of Tactile Time collage.* © *Roxana Moroşanu.*

2016). However, elements of these methods could be explored and adapted so as to suit other research topics related to the experience of time, or the use of technology, within the home.

Self-reporting methods

Other creative methods have been developed to enable exploration of participant's home life without the presence of the researcher. 'Probe' kits can be sent to or left with participants to be completed in their own time. The cultural probe method was first introduced by Bill Gaver and colleagues as part of the Presence Project (Gaver, Hooker and Dunne 2001). The concept was inspired by space probes that were sent off from earth to gather data from distant planets. Deliberately intriguing activities involving drawing, collaging and photo taking were used to gain insight into the lives of the older adults at the heart of the project. Gaver never meant for probes to be formally analysed – they were ways to provoke and inspire. The technique has been adapted by others to provide a way to collect more structured data from participants (see for example Haines et al. 2007). It's interesting to note that participants do not always engage fully with probe activities. The design teams within two projects through which we undertook design research in homes – CALEBRE (Vadodaria et al. 2010) and CCC (Lilley et al. 2010) – left self-report materials in the home containing creative activities designed to help understand how participants made themselves comfortable at home. However many packs were only partially completed by participants with some guiltily retrieved from drawers when the researcher returned to collect them. This has led us to reflect on the use of self-reflect methods in the home. Asking participants to remember to fill in diary entries repeatedly (however visually engaging the materials are), for example, is unlikely to succeed. In contrast a 'mission pack' containing a limited number of short tasks used by Haines et al. (2007) worked very well. Like Moroşanu's collaging activity described above, it only required one focused period of time from participants. Interestingly the older adults in the CCC project found the activities in the self-report pack rather daunting, reflecting similar findings from Burrows et al. (2015) who found some older adults hesitant to complete self-report tasks with a disposable camera. Creative self-report activities should therefore be used with care within studies of the home; although potentially able to provide rich insight into home life, the time commitment and demands on participants need to be carefully considered.

In a number of studies of the home, we have asked participants to capture their experiences of home at times when we were not present. This allowed us to explore family life without the disturbance of our presence in the home as researchers or guests. A different approach to self-capture is seen in Kevin Mercer's study of media use in the home (Mercer et al. 2014). Participants were asked to wear a small camera and to begin recording whenever they watched video-based content on any device. After careful coaching and practice sessions, the participants successfully captured short video clips of their media use, which were later discussed and reflected upon within focus groups outside of the home. Andrea Burris (Burris, 2014) took this approach further by asking participants to wear a Sensecam lifelogging camera to capture how participants wind down after work in the home. The camera is designed to take a still image every ten seconds with no intervention needed from the participant once they had activated the camera. This method successfully captured the mundane comfort-making activities and routines of participants, many of which they would normally struggle to recall. Again the method is most powerful when participants are given the opportunity to reflect on the camera footage together with the researcher. Since Burris's study was completed, smaller- and higher-resolution lifelogging cameras have become available (e.g. the Narrative Clip [http://getnarrative.com]), which the authors, among others, have begun to experiment with to provide new ways to study the home.

Self-interviewing methods: The Five Cups of Tea video method

Self-interviewing methods can be regarded as a specific type of self-reporting method, as they involve the participants engaging with the research questions in their own time and space. One of the first developments and conceptualizations of the self-interview was in the field of memory studies (Keightley, Pickering and Allett 2012). In a research project looking at the use of digital media to foster acts of remembering, the self-interview method was introduced in order to give research participants more time for self-reflection than a standard interview would normally do (Keightley, Pickering and Allett 2012: 509). When voice recording oneself at home, one is able to stop, pause and continue whenever they wish, and to play, delete and restart their recording. This gives research participants more control over their involvement in the research, as well as the opportunity to take their time to explore their thoughts on a specific topic with no pressure to respond immediately.

In Roxana's research, the development of the Five Cups of Tea method was inspired by this approach to the self-interview as a way to foster and facilitate self-reflection. As the name of the method suggests, the everyday practice of having a cup of tea – that was culturally situated in the British middle-class settings where the research was conducted – provided a particular temporal and

FIGURE 5.10 *Still image from a video recording of the Five Cups of Tea series.* © *Roxana Moroşanu.*

spatial framework for addressing questions. In order to employ this method, the research participants were given a small video camera (a Sony Bloggie), together with an information pack that included five sets of questions, and they were asked to video record themselves preparing and having a cup of tea, and responding to the associated questions, for five times during the course of a week. This timeline provided enough flexibility, while giving a focus to the week and keeping interest for the task. Some participants chose the same cup of tea occasion, such as the first morning cup, every day, while others chose to do some of their recordings in a row during a Saturday – or over the whole weekend – showing the changes in their activities from cup to cup.

As Roxana's research looked at the qualities of time in domestic settings, this method was designed so as to provide a different entry point into this topic. The Five Cups of Tea provided a means of looking at moments of solitude while not intruding or interrupting them. The questions to be responded to while having a cup of tea were chosen and formulated so as to enhance the mindfulness of these moments, and to foster self-reflection: from asking participants to describe the taste and the feeling of having a cup of tea to someone who never tried it, to questions about personal hopes and dreams and about experiences of parenting. The cup of tea breaks were also situated within the flow of the day's activities. For each cup, the research participants were asked to share what they were doing before the break and what they were planning to do afterwards. While revealing the affordances of a cup of tea break to reorganize one's thoughts and prepare them for the next set of tasks, these questions also brought up interesting insights about the different temporal qualities of various modes of activity, such as the situation of intermixing tasks.

The visual content of the recordings was left to the choice of the participants. Some employed the video camera as a witness to their experience of having a cup of tea, filming the setting and objects around them that were part of having that experience: the cup of tea, a busy table top, their phone or other devices and objects they would use during the break. Other participants turned the recording device towards themselves when answering the questions and talked directly to the camera. In each and every case, though, the video camera kept them company in their cup of tea breaks, capturing the corporeal image (MacDougall 2006) of the person filming, together with a few non-propositional insights about how different people experience their moments of solitude.

Apart from the context of this specific research on everyday temporalities and energy demand, the Five Cups of Tea video method could be adapted and employed in many other qualitative research scenarios, addressing questions related to embodied ways of knowing and to modes of inner expression.

Video diaries: The Evening Times video recording method

Similar to self-interviewing methods, video diaries can be employed in situations when the presence of a researcher would be intrusive and when giving participants a longer period of time to engage with the research questions can trigger a different type of insights. Unlike self-interviews, video diaries do not normally employ a pack of specific questions to be responded to in each and every recording, but there is more flexibility regarding what can be filmed and shared. For example, in their work on family traditions, Muir and Mason (2012) handed out camcorders and asked the people taking part in the research to record their Christmas Day. The participants were able to decide what moments and situations to film, with no other specific requirements regarding the length of filming either. This meant that, in the end, all participants filmed other events alongside Christmas Day but that were nonetheless part of what Christmas holidays meant for them.

In Roxana's research, the Evening Times video recording method was developed as a way of exploring situations when family members spent time together, or what is called 'family time'. The participants were given a small video camera (a Sony Bloggie) for a week, and they were asked to record their family for a few evenings by passing the camera on, so that by the end of the week each family member would have filmed the others for at least one evening. In this way we made sure that all the viewpoints over 'family time' were represented and that we did not give disproportionate control to one family member over filming the others. We wanted to know, specifically, about the ways in which digital devices, such as laptops, tablets and smartphones, were employed as part of 'family time', and we asked the participants to video record such moments when the other family members used their individual devices.

The resulting materials could not have been more heterogeneous. With one family member in charge of each evening, the recordings not only differed, in content and filming style, between the family participants, but also between family members. Some people filmed a series of several clips, showing the evolution and the changes in the evening, while others preferred recording one long continuous video. Some moved with the camera, going from room to room, in order to follow the other family members and their digital devices, while others placed the camera still in one spot and continued their evening activities.

However, in all these situations, the camcorder became part of the digital technologies that the participants normally used in their evenings at home. The content of the video recordings, as well as the way in which the camera was used in relation to the other family members, brought new insights about forms of sociality that involve the use of technology. As it was one of the digital devices employed in these situations, the camcorder became not just a way of representing what can be called 'family time with digital media', but an actual part of the enactment of these moments.

We did not predict that this method would fit so well in our participants' domestic activities, and in relation to the research questions that it was designed to address. This insight invites new considerations over the potential and the roles of digital methods when employed as part of research that addresses the ways in which people use digital technologies.

Summing up

In this chapter we have reviewed and discussed a series of design ethnography research methods for understanding the home. Often the methods described are used in relation to each other, or as in the case of interviews and video tours and re-enactments, can blur into each other as the research encounter progresses. To maintain a distinction between the different activities, it is useful to consider what, in each case, forms the main narrative or probe guiding the encounter. For example, the use of the tour of the home puts the materiality and sensoriality of home at the centre of the encounter, the activity-based encounters focus on the activity itself as the main probe through which researcher and participant seek to learn together, and the interview put the interaction between researcher, participant, and whatever other things are brought into that context by the participant at the core of the site of investigation.

These methods have been tested across a series of projects and, as we have noted, have informed some of the ideas that we have discussed in Chapters 2–4. Research methods for researching homes are most effective when tailored towards different projects. That is, the methods discussed above are not presented to be used as they are, but are ready for readers to adapt or to use as inspiration for future projects. Above we have also given a good number of references to other works where these methods and their specific in situ applications are discussed in more detail.

6

Homes in translation

This chapter sums up the implications of the frameworks and techniques discussed in this book for future research and design agendas for the home. We first focus on the question of how such approaches are usefully communicated and implemented in ways that can have impact in the world. We then reflect on the significance of bringing together ethnography and design in a contemporary context where conceptualizations of home are shifting in particular ways. We also reflect on the question of how future homes might be conceptualized, and how a design ethnography approach might both mitigate the myths of future lives that are constructed by the narratives of the technological possible and question of what a home might mean in the future. Finally, we suggest where research that brings together design, ethnography and concepts of home might travel in its own future.

Making impact through ethnography and design in homes

In this book, while discussing ethnographic and design research and practice in homes, we have also presented an applied agenda for this work, rather than one for simply understanding better how people live in homes. Much of the work we have discussed in the previous chapters has been research that is orientated towards change-making in some contexts since this is the focus of design more broadly. Another example is that Sarah Pink's work on homes, including that published in her book *Home Truths* (2004), *Situating Everyday Life* (2012) and in the film *Laundry Lives* (Pink and Astari 2015), was one of the outcomes of research developed in partnership with Unilever. Often this research has been, on the one hand, engaged in an environmental sustainability agenda, in which sense it aims to have a wider impact on the world, and in accordance with discourses and orientations that might be shared with particular government, organizations or movements. On the other hand, simultaneously our work has involved researching everyday life and in some cases prototyping or creating practical interventions for change in everyday life contexts. It is not our aim here to provide an instruction manual for impact. However, we are interested in exploring the ways in which work that is specifically focused on the home might travel out of academic research contexts and into public and applied domains, or become a form of public pedagogy. This seems particularly important given that simultaneous to our own and others' academic research that problematizes roles that technology might play in our future homes are emerging technologically based discourses about smart home futures that our findings would contest (as is discussed further later in this chapter).

Throughout this book we have referred to the text, images and video clips that are presented on our Energy and Digital Living website, which was developed with the company Paper Giant (their contribution is discussed on the website). The website was one of the outputs of the wider interdisciplinary LEEDR project and brings together the ethnography and design research strands of the project along with offering a video archive. The website was intended to be used by multiple audiences: for teaching ethnographic and design disciplines; to describe and show our methods and approach to other researchers who are interested in undertaking similar work, adapted to their own projects; to demonstrate our approach and what it can achieve to potential research partners from other academic disciplines or from outside academia; for us to show in presentations; for other researchers to potentially use to analyse our video clips in other ways and for other exercises; and finally for a wider interested public to be able to access our findings and outputs. However Energy and Digital Living was also an experiment in web-based dissemination of research and was in this sense also intended to advance the genre of project websites beyond conventional sites that report on progress, publications or blog findings (see, for example, discussions in Pink and Abram 2015). In this sense we aimed to generate a place where users could engage more deeply with our research process, experience and materials, as well as to provide a framework through which to be able to present the work and aspects of it. Likewise the *Laundry Lives* documentary website is intended to support pedagogical uses of the film – both as a form of public pedagogy and for possible uses of the film as a probe for design studios. Indeed several of the examples from the sites discussed in the earlier chapters of this book often form part of presentations derived from the materials on the site; these have been selected specifically because they enable us to make wider points about how people live in homes, how ethnographic processes often play out and the types of knowledge and knowing that a sensory ethnography approach produces.

Significantly, research in homes has implications beyond purely academic audiences. This includes a range of different types of business and public sector and NGO-type organizations, concerned with, for example, digital technologies, domestic products, domestic services and more. For example in our own work, ongoing collaboration with the UK sustainable development organization Forum for the Future has provided the opportunity to partner with businesses to explore sustainable futures using materials from the Energy and Digital Living website alongside established business-oriented futures methodologies. Indeed many people now access services in their homes that they would have conventionally accessed in a high-street branch, store or other outlet. Given this context where there is a broad interest in, and need to understand, the home, it is important to seek new and effective ways to reach them. Digital and visual media offer one possibility.

Design, ethnography and reconceptualizing home

In the preceding chapters of this book we have outlined how design and ethnography can be brought together to develop new approaches to understanding homes and processes of change-making in homes. This approach, we argue, also needs to be extended to play a further role in a world where home is, as we have outlined in Chapter 1, a mainstay of everyday life. There in our discussion of how home might be defined, we have highlighted that home might be a feeling rather than a house as such, a place of work (both for working at home and for working in other people's homes), a place of gendered or other types of power, friction and tension, and more.

We also discussed how different approaches to home have developed across a range of different disciplines, which have focused on different elements of home, including its material culture, spatiality, sensoriality, atmospheres and its relevance to migrant and diasporic identities, and more. The home has also been seen, particularly in our own work, as a site for engagement with environmental sustainability agendas through use of digital technologies. However, much of this existing research about homes and everyday lives in homes is undertaken in the established academic disciplines – that is, it tends to be discussed in the context of critical debates within disciplines and published in journals read by scholars with similar critical and empirical interests. Our argument is for making

FIGURE 6.1 *Home is also often a workplace, as it is for research participants who work from home.* © *LEEDR.*

stronger connections between such empirical and theoretical work and the insights that it can offer for change-making through design. There are a range of different areas in which such approaches could be applied in that bodies of work on home are becoming increasingly developed in a current academic context where questions of futures, uncertainty and impact are emerging as important concerns, for instance, in human geography, anthropology and sociology. Here by way of example we reflect on two of these, but invite readers to imagine others. The first is the migration and home, and the second refers to how other people's homes become a (frequently ambiguous) workplace for some.

In Chapter 2 we discussed how these future-oriented approaches were emerging in the form of discussions of expectations, aspirations, imaginations and futures in these disciplines. At the same time, in the material culture studies tradition, the work of Petridou (2001), Horst (2006, 2011), Pink and Postill (2016) has shown that researching migrants' homemaking both in their places of origin and in their places of destination provides insights into how people improvise when creating everyday domestic environments that bring together the values, moralities, routines, expectations, materialities, technologies and infrastructures of different cultures and nation states. These works have two layers of significance in relation to a design ethnography approach to home. First, they provide us with deep understandings of what home does and can mean, and often also because migrants are people explicitly in movement in ways that are not only physical but also material and aspirational, such studies provide us with a sense of how they imagine and plan for their own futures, and importantly, why they do so in the ways that they do. Such studies provide excellent examples of improvisory ways of doing and being. However they also show the difficulties, conflicts and struggles that are part of migration – both materially and emotionally. They as such raise the question of how we might better design for and with migrant groups, that is, they invite us to ask how a design ethnography approach might support processes of making homes, and a sense of home, in such contexts. Existing research in such fields has explored how members of migrant and diasporic groups make home, and has involved art-based research and intervention (e.g. in the work of Tolia-Kelly 2010). Yet, by developing design-oriented approaches, such understandings might be taken further to ask new questions. For instance, how might design ethnography interventions be developed to enable new forms of well-being among temporary migrants such as international students (see Pink and Postill 2016), as well as for newly arrived refugees? In this context readers might also ask what a book that has focused mainly on examples of how people live in their homes-houses in the United Kingdom, Australia, Spain and Indonesia has to do with the situations of people for whom homes are no longer houses, perhaps because they have lost them due to war, disasters such as earthquakes or other weather-related events, fires and other causes. We do not claim to be able to extend the scope and relevance of all the arguments made in this book to such contexts. However we do propose that the concepts of temporality, environment and movement offer a framework that might be more widely applied; we would argue for using this as a starting point to explore what might matter in such other contexts, but always with the proviso that it is also a framework to remould.

In a contemporary context where there is a growing ageing population of people living (often alone) in the homes in certain national contexts, and an increase in online shopping, there is a growing workforce of people for whom other people's homes are a workplace. Simultaneously there is a growing population of people who work from their own homes. As various of the research projects discussed in this book have shown (e.g. Pink, Horst et al. 2016; Pink, Morgan and Dainty 2015; Fergusson 2009, 2010; Pink and Astari 2015), the concepts of temporality, environment and movement have also proved to be useful prisms through which to understand the experiences of these people. Indeed, we might also begin to consider how and where design ethnographies of homes should not simply always be thought of as enabling particular ways for people to live in homes, but as enabling the ways in which the home is also a workplace in such ways, and how its status as a workplace will shift over the life course.

There are a number of potential ways in which design ethnographies of homes might go about seeking to make interventions in everyday life, which could support householders as they seek to live differently or to accomplish particular tasks or goals in their everyday lives. As part of our LEEDR project we developed a series of design concepts that sought to play such roles in everyday life in the home, which are presented on the Energy and Digital Living website and discussed in other published contexts (e.g. Pink, Leder Mackley et al. 2016). More broadly, we propose that possibilities for future design ethnography research might include the design of objects but would also be focused towards the design of services, digital interventions, processes, ways of generating atmospheres and other non-tangible but important elements of the everyday. The design concepts developed in LEEDR project took a first step towards this, in ways that acknowledged the digital–material–sensory relationships that constitute homes but that did not depend on any assumptions about what smart homes will necessarily be. Here we present two examples of how such an approach to the home that engages with the ethnographic research through the concepts of temporality, environment and movement might be mobilized into digital interventions for sustainable living in the home.

The Future Self

The Future Self concept developed by Garrath Wilson imagined an app where householders could commune with their future selves when thinking through their future plans for their home. This app engaged directly with the temporality

FIGURE 6.2 *As outlined in the Design in Practice section of the Energy and Digital Living website: 'Future/Self is an opportunity to bend time. Future/Self is an app that allows you to commune with your own future self; be guided with your own seasoned words on your own big life decisions. When should I have a baby and what do I need to do to be ready? Is now the right time to invest in solar panels? What will happen if I let my parents move in with me? Through Future/Self, we have explored how the concept of "life stages" and "bending time" can be used to pro-actively inform an individual or family on an activity, perhaps in order to be more time efficient or to save energy' (http://energyanddigitalliving.com/design-in-practice/). Further details of the design of Future/Self can be found in an online PDF here: http://energyanddigitalliving.com/wp-content/uploads/2014/09/FutureSelf.pdf. © LEEDR.*

of home and resonates with concepts discussed in Chapter 2, including that of the project of home and the notion of hope in the way we imagine future homes, with specific reference to energy use.

Anima

The Anima concept developed by Garrath Wilson, Val Mitchell and William Godfrey responded to the insight that when the routines and rhythms of family life become busy, then energy is likely to be used less efficiently in the home.

FIGURE 6.3 *The Anima concept: Anima is a proxy for the heartbeat of the home, designed to draw the household into considering the energy use of the home in terms of its 'health' or 'fitness', rather than using abstract energy or ecological metrics, such as Kilowatts or carbon units – units which have been shown time and again to be intangible to the everyday user. Further details of the design of Anima can be found in an online PDF: http://energyanddigitalliving.com/wp-content/uploads/2014/09/ Anima.pdf. © LEEDR.*

'Anima' proposed that digital technology could be used to create an ambient display of a home's heartbeat that would subtly signal to a family when life was stressful and encourage them to slow down. This reflection would be in the moment triggered by the stressed and dynamically pulsing 'heart' shape. Thus, this design concept resonated with the notions of the routines and rhythms of home, discussed as part of the understanding of the temporalities of home outlined in Chapter 2. It also engages with the importance of the emotional and sensory elements of the atmosphere of home – or the idea that home should feel 'right', which is advanced in Chapter 3.

Both of these design concepts, therefore, offer ways in which an intangible element such as energy can be made tangible or concrete in everyday life, by recognizing how and where its use is entangled with the sensory and emotional ways in which people experience and imagine their everyday lives at home in the present and the future. They are intended here as an example of how design ethnographic concepts can travel into design interventions in ways that enable such interventions to draw directly from in-depth understandings of participants' experiential worlds. These understandings, as we have emphasized in Chapter 5, are best created from engagements and encounters with participants that go beyond superficial treatments of their worlds and instead seek to acknowledge the unspoken, felt and performative dimensions of how life is lived and imagined. Our examples have focused on energy use in homes. This offers a useful illustration of the approach because while energy demand research is a very populated research field, it is also a field of study that has been little engaged with through ethnography until recently. It is particularly interesting in the context of our discussion here, since it specifically deals with an invisible resource, which is only made material or visible through its relationships with other materialities, digital technologies and media and human activities and feelings, and as such our design interventions needed to be likewise interwoven with these elements. The same principle, we propose, could be adapted to research in other related fields of research in the home, whereas in this example, the relationships between the different processes and things that are implicated in the home need to be acknowledged in the making of interventions towards change.

As these forms of relatedness are increasingly acknowledged, new types of interdisciplinary frameworks will be needed in order to bring together the research materials and findings that enable us to make connections between things and processes of different qualities and affordances, as well as between different types of disciplinary knowledge. For example, the design team within LEEDR initially found it challenging to respond to thinking about the home in terms of these interwoven experiential elements. Framing and reframing of problem and solution spaces is core to the conceptual design process and key to creativity (Dorst and Cross 2001). Design research studies in the home, therefore, have often tended to focus on understanding a known problem, for example, how to reduce the energy demand associated with the use of cold appliances in the home (Tang and Bhamra 2012). The design ethnography approach at the core of this book, however, encouraged a more systemic response from designers that embraces the complexity of the sensory and experiential environment of home. An initial response to this complexity was to adopt a predominantly empathic response where insights into possible futures could be derived from in-depth yet unstructured immersion into the ethnographic research with the goal of discovering unexpected insights into home life to be reframed as design opportunities. However, there are other possibilities for working in a more structured way. For instance, a more systematic approach was proposed and explored within LEEDR through the development of the PORTS (people, objects and resources through time and space) methodology (Wilson et al. 2014). PORTS focused on understanding the intersections and impacts of people, objects and resources in relation to their movement over time and through the home (time and space). PORTS sought to identify novel routes to intervention rather than to create 'solutions' to problems, but our work with it also revealed that it was difficult to resolve how to manage the complexity of the relationships between the five elements it focused on, leaving opportunities for further investigation in this field of methodological process.

Researching future homes

The question of the future home is complex, and needs to account for a number of factors, including how the digital materiality of homes will emerge in relation to their architecture, the processes by which they are designed and built, their functionality and the ways that people will experience this. One of the themes that has dominated the way that future homes are imagined in our present is the smart home debate. We frame this as a 'debate' in acknowledgement of scholars like Strengers, whose work has shown us that the smart home question needs to be debated and critiqued rather than simply assumed as given, and like Lanzeni, whose work shows us that smart technology design itself needs to be interrogated (Lanzeni 2016; Lanzeni and Ardevol 2017). Generally, according to Strengers, a smart home has been defined as a home that has computing systems that can anticipate residents' needs (Strengers 2016). As such it offers a series of technological possibilities and for some it is an assumed future reality. For example, in Intel's 'International Internet of Things Smart Home Survey', it was 'found that 77 per cent of respondents believe smart homes will be as common in 2025 as smartphones are today' (https://newsroom.intel.com/news-releases/intel-securitys-international-internet-of-things-smart-home-survey/ (accessed 30 July 2016)). However, as Strengers has also pointed out, much existing research and prediction about smart homes comes from technological disciplines, which tends to be 'utopian' and does not account for 'users' of or dwellers in smart homes, or for how people really live out life in homes (Strengers 2016). The latter is one of the areas we have set out to explore in this book. That is, rather than to consider the smartness of the home, to understand how people are already smart. As the findings of the various ethnographic studies discussed in this book reveal, and as Strengers' critiques imply the smart home is unlikely to emerge as a smooth technological future vision. It is rather likely to be a messy domain, where ongoing technological possibility, development and design intersect with markets (see also Lanzeni and Ardevol 2017). It will be a place where human improvisation and everyday perceptions and anticipations of near and far futures make home a human project that is continually challenged by the contingencies of everyday life and unexpected configurations of processes and things. The home will also be a practical site where people's expectations and actions connect to what they already know and value; as we have seen in Chapter 3, the problems of energy demand reduction and efficient use of sunlight can sometimes easily be resolved with simple crafted technologies, like the stick. Another key theme in future homes is the notion of the environmentally sustainable home, which, as Strengers (2016) also noted, is often bound up the smart home concept, whereby smart homes are seen as solutions that will lead to sustainability. In the future we might still need to ask ourselves: why do you need a smart home if you have a stick? The utopian vision of smart homes also fails to account for how future homes will be constituted and what the digital materiality of this might feel like. Therefore we would also call for researchers to be wary of the dominance of this image and to explore further renderings of how the digital, material and social will constitute future homes. For example, the Intel report cited above goes on to note that many people were worried about data security in smart homes in that 'almost all respondents out of the 9000 are concerned with personal data theft. This leads to another interesting finding that innovation in smart homes will lure consumers and specifically those targeting the security angle of smart homes' (http://www.dispatchtribunal.com/consumers-may-be-willing-to-compromise-on-privacy-to-adopt-smart-home-tech/20398/ (accessed 30 July 2016)).

This leads us to further considerations for thinking about future homes. They are likely to be data-producing and data-using environments, just as much as our smartphones, wearables and other contemporary digital technologies are in the middle of the second decade of the twenty-first century. The introduction of smart technologies into homes also has other implications for future homes, which are similar to those that have been encountered in research about smartphones and wearables (e.g. Pink and Fors 2017) whereby data both frames and is shaped by how people live out their everyday life routines, the contingencies of everyday life, and their anxieties and aspirations. This has implications for how we will research the digital materiality of homes. Yet it does not necessarily change the set of three principles that we have engaged to structure this book: temporality, environment and movement. For example: when we consider the temporalities of home, we might be considering future, anticipated or hoped for uses of data; when we ask what people do to make their homes feel right, we might be asking them how they use or experience data, and how they use their data to make improvements in their homes, how they feel about the data they produce by living in their homes being harvested by others and how they act in relation to this; and we may be concerned with how data and human movement in the home are co-implicated. Such contexts and issues call for a 'data ethnographies' approach – that is, an approach that accounts for how people experience living in worlds (and in this case homes) where their everyday environments are at least in part constituted

by the production, use and presence of digital data (as developed at www.
dataethnographies.com). This, we propose, is a key question for future design
ethnography in homes.

Future homes research

In this book we have outlined a set of starting points for understanding and
considering interventions in homes. We have shown through our discussions
of existing research findings, processes and methods how these can be
applied and the insights that they can generate. However research is always
ongoing: once a project is completed and publications go to press, there
are always new questions, issues and projects raised and undertaken, and
that lie waiting to be taken up. Thus, of course, there are further theoretical
and methodological implications for the field of researching and designing
with homes, which, we argue, need to form part of the upcoming research
agendas in this field. There are ways that we might think about this in relation
to digital technology and design in the home, but that are not simply informed
by the lure of the technologically possible, but rather that are rooted in design
ethnographic research. For example our research has shown that attention
to temporality, environment and movement all lead us to useful and new
insights towards design in homes. This has been materialized in the form of
the prototype digital design interventions presented on our Energy and Digital
Living website and in the possible use of Pink and Astari's *Laundry Lives* film
as a design studio probe (as detailed on the film's website). In these works the
future of homes and the role of design in working towards the home as a site
for environmental sustainability are evident. These future-focused outcomes
are also congruent with recent theoretical and methodological moves, which,
we argue, together, imply possibilities for next steps in this field of research
and practice and raise a series of key questions:

1 How do designers of 'smart homes' or of smart technologies for
   homes conceptualize the interplay between users, buildings and
   technology?

2 What are the actual, rather than assumed, implications of the
   technological possibilities for future homes when they are situated in
   relation to everyday life human activity?

3 How do people explicitly and tacitly consider and make futures when
   they make and imagine their homes on an everyday basis across
   different cultural contexts?

4　If movement is central to the way people experience, make and imagine homes, how will they move on into their futures, and what will accompany them and how?

5　If the environments of home and the ways they feel are important for how people engage with their homes, what should future homes feel like, and how can the making of such 'feels' of home work towards values, such as sustainability, equity and responsibility?

References

Abram, S. (2017), 'Contemporary Obsessions with Time and the Promise of the Future', in J. F. Salazar, S. Pink, A. Irving and J. Sjoberg (eds), *Future Anthropologies*, London: Bloomsbury.

Adam, B. and C. Groves (2007), *Future Matters: Action, Knowledge, Ethics*, Leiden: Brill Academic Publishing.

Akama, Y. and A. Prendiville (2013), 'A Phenomenological View to Co-Designing Services', *Swedish Design Research Journal*, 1(13): 29–40.

Amit, V. (2000), 'The University as Panopticon: Moral Claims and Attacks on Academic Freedom', in M. Strathern (ed.), *Audit Cultures: Anthropological Studies in Accountability*, London: Routledge.

Anderson, B. (2009), 'Affective Atmospheres', *Emotion, Space and Society*, 2: 77–81.

Anderson, B. (2010), 'Preemption, Precaution, Preparedness: Anticipatory Action and Future Geographies', *Progress in Human Geography*, 34(6): 777–98.

Ardevol, E. and D. Lanzeni (2017), 'Futures Come to Us: An Ethnographic Conceptualization of Building up Common Futures Among Technology Makers', in J. F. Salazar, S. Pink, A. Irving and J. Sjoberg (eds), *Future Anthropologies*, London: Bloomsbury.

Bagnoli, A. (2009), 'Beyond the Standard Interview: The Use of Graphic Elicitation and Arts-Based Methods', *Qualitative Research*, 9(5): 547–70.

Bech-Danielsen, C. (2012), 'The Kitchen: An Architectural Mirror of Everyday Life and Societal Development', *Journal of Civil Engineering and Architecture*, 6(4): 457–69.

Bille, M. (2014), 'Lighting Up Cosy Atmospheres in Denmark', *Emotion, Space and Society*, http://dx.doi.org/10.1016/j.emospa.2013.12.008.

Bille, M. (2015a), 'Hazy Worlds: Atmospheric Ontologies in Denmark', *Anthropological Theory*, 15(3): 257–74.

Bille, M. (2015b), 'Lighting Up Cosy Atmospheres in Denmark', *Emotion, Space and Society*, 15: 56–63.

Bille, M. (2017), 'Ecstatic Things: The Power of Light in Shaping Bedouin Homes', *Home Cultures*, 14(1).

Bille, M. and T. Sørensen (2007), 'An Anthropology of Luminosity: The Agency of Light', *Journal of Material Culture*, 12(3): 263–84.

Bille, M., P. Bjerregaard and T. Flohr Sørensen (2014), 'Staging Atmospheres: Materiality, Culture, and the Texture of the In-Between', *Emotion, Space and Society*, 15: 31–38.

Bissell, D. (2010), 'Passenger Mobilities: Affective Atmospheres and the Sociality of Public Transport', *Environment and Planning D*, 28: 270–89.

Blunt, A. and A. Varley (2004), 'Introduction: Geographies of Home', *Cultural Geographies*, 11: 3–6.

Blunt, A. and R. Dowling (2006), *Home*, Abingdon: Routledge.

Bødker, S. (2006), 'When second wave HCI meets third wave challenges', In *Proceedings of 4th Nordic Conference HCI*, 1–8.

Böhme, G. (1993), 'Atmosphere as the Fundamental Concept of a New Aesthetics', *Thesis Eleven* 36: 113–26.

Böhme, G. (2013), 'The Art of the Stage Set as a Paradigm for an Aesthetics of Atmospheres', *Ambiances: International Journal of Sensory Environment, Architecture and Urban Space* [online]. Published online 10 February 2013. http://ambiances.revues.org/315.

Bräuchler, B. and J. Postill (eds) (2010), *Theorising Media and Practice*, Oxford: Berghahn.

Brickell, K. (2012), '"Mapping" and "Doing" Critical Geographies of Home', *Progress in Human Geography*, 36(2): 225–44.

Brickell, K. (2014), '"Plates in a Basket will Rattle": Marital Dissolution and Home "Unmaking" in Contemporary Cambodia', *Geoforum* 51: 262–72.

Brown, N. and M. Michael (2003), 'A Sociology of Expectations: Retrospecting Prospects and Prospecting Retrospects', *Technology Analysis & Strategic Management*, 15(1): 3–18.

Bucchli, V. (2013), *An Anthropology of Architecture*, London: Bloomsbury.

Burrows, A., V. Mitchell and C. Nicolle (2011), 'Designing in Social Benefits', In *Include 2011 Proceedings. 6th International Conference on Inclusive Design: The Role of Inclusive Design in Making Social Innovation Happen*, Royal College of Art, London, UK, 18–20 April.

Burrows, A., V. Mitchell and C. A.Nicolle (2016), 'Let's Spend Some Time Together: Exploring the Out-of-Box Experience of Technology for Older Adults', *International Journal of Mobile Human Computer Interaction*, 8(2): 69–82.

Buur, J., T. Binder and E. Brandt (2000), 'Taking Video Beyond "Hard Data" in User Centred Design', In *PDC 2000 Proceedings of the Participatory Design Conference*, New York, NY, 28 November to 1 December 2000, 21–9.

Cefkin, M. (ed.) (2009), *Ethnography and the Corporate Encounter*, Oxford: Berghahn.

Chevalier, S. (1995), 'The Anthropology of an Apparent Banality: A Comparative Study', *Cambridge Anthropology*, 19(3): 25–39.

Chevalier, S. (1998), 'From Woollen Carpet to Grass Carpet: Bridging House and Garden in an Burb', in D. Miller (ed.), *Material Cultures*, London: Routledge.

Christensen, T. H. and I. Røpke (2010), 'Can Practice Theory Inspire Studies of Icts in Everyday Life?', in B. Bräuchler and J. Postill (eds), *Theorising Media and Practice*, 233–56, Oxford: Berghahn Books.

Clarke, A (2001), 'The Aesthetics of Social Aspiration', in D. Miller (ed.), *Home Possessions*, Oxford: Berg.

Clarke, A. (2009), 'The Contemporary Interior: Trajectories of Biography and Style', in B. Martin and P. Sparke (eds), *Designing the Modern Interior*, Oxford: Berg.

Clarke, A. (ed.) (2010), *Design Anthropology: Object Culture in the 21st Century*, Wien/New York: Springer Verlag.

Clifford, J. and G. Marcus (eds) (1986), *Writing Culture: The Poetics and Politics of Ethnography*, Berkeley: University of California Press.

Cordelois, A. (2010), 'Using Digital Technology for Collective Ethnographic Observation: An Experiment on "Coming Home"', *Social Science Information*, 49: 445–63.

Couldry, N. (2012), *Media, Society, World: Social Theory and Digital Media Practice*, Cambridge: Polity Press.

Crabtree, A. and T. Rodden (2004), 'Domestic Routines and Design for the Home', *Computer Supported Cooperative Work*, 13: 191–220. doi:10.1023/B:COSU.0000045712.26840.a4

DeSilvey, C. (2006), 'Observed Decay: Telling Stories with Mutable Things', *Journal of Material Culture*, 11(3): 318–38.

Dixon, H., V. A. Mitchell and S. D. Harker (2003), 'Mobile Phone Games', in D. McDonagh, P. Hekkert, J. V. Erp and D. Gyi (eds), *Design and Emotion*, 256–61, CRC Press.

Domínguez Rubio, F. (2016), 'On the Discrepancy Between Objects and Things: An Ecological Approach', *Journal of Material Culture*, 21(1): 59–86.

Dourish, P. (2001a), *Where The Action Is: The Foundations Of Embodied Interaction*, Boston: MIT Press.

Dourish, P. (2001b), 'Seeking a Foundation for Context-Aware Computing', *Human-Computer Interaction*, 16: 2–3.

Dourish, P. (2006), 'Implications for Design', CHI 2006, ACM Press, 541–50.

Dourish, P. (2010), 'HCI and Environmental Sustainability: The Politics of Design and the Design of Politics', In *Proceedings of Designing Interactive Systems* (DIS 2010), 16–20 August, Aarhus, Denmark.

Dourish, P. and G. Bell (2011), *Divining a Digital Future: Mess And Mythology in Ubiquitous Computing*, Boston: MIT Press.

Dovey, K (1999), *Framing Places: Mediating Power in Built Form*, London: Routledge.

Drazin, A. (2001), 'A Man *Will* Get Furnished: Wood and Domesticity in Urban Romania', in D. Miller (ed.), *Home Possessions*, Oxford: Berg.

Duffy, M. and G. Waitt (2013), 'Home Sounds: Experiential Practices and Performativities of Hearing and Listening', *Social & Cultural Geography*, 14(4): 466–81.

Dyck, I, P. Konto, J. Angus and P. McKeever (2005), 'The Home as a Site for Long-Term Care: Meanings and Management of Bodies and Spaces', *Health & Place*, 11:173–85.

Edensor, T and S. Sumartojo (2015), 'Introduction: Designing atmospheres', *Visual Communication*, 14(2): 251–66.

Ehn, B. and O. Lofgren (2010), *The Secret World of Doing Nothing*, California: University of California Press.

Energy saving trust (n.d.), 'Energy Efficient Lighting', http://www.energysavingtrust.org.uk/home-energy-efficiency/lighting, accessed 21 June 2016.

Fabian J (1983), *Time and the Other: How Anthropology Makes its Object*, New York: Columbia University Press.

Ferguson, H. (2008), 'Liquid Social Work: Welfare Interventions as Mobile Practices', *British Journal of Social Work*, 38: 561–79.

Ferguson, H. (2009), 'Performing Child Protection: Home Visiting, Movement and the Struggle to Reach the Abused Child', *Child & Family Social Work*, 14(4): 471–80.

Ferguson, H. (2010), 'Walks, Home Visits and Atmospheres: Risk and the Everyday Practices and Mobilities of Social Work and Child Protection', *British Journal of Social Work*, 40(4): 1100–17.doi: 10.1093/bjsw/bcq015.

Garvey, P. (2001), 'Organised Disorder: Moving Furniture in Norweigan Homes', in D. Miller (ed.), *Home Possessions*, Oxford: Berg.

Garvey, P. (2010), 'Consuming IKEA and Inspiration as Material Form', in A. Clarke (ed.), *Design Anthropology: Object Culture in the 21st Century*, Wien, New York: Springer Verlag.

Gaver, W., A. Boucher, S. Pennington and B. Walker (2004), 'Cultural Probes and the Value of Uncertainty', *Interactions*, 11(5): 53–6.

Goggin, G. and L. Hjorth (2014), 'Introduction: Mobile Media Research – State of the Art', in G. Goggin and L. Hjorth (eds), *The Routledge Companion to Mobile Media*, 1–8, Routledge, United Kingdom.

Gram-Hanssen, K. (2007), 'Teenage Consumption of Cleanliness: How to Make it Sustainable?', *Sustainability: Science, Practice, & Policy*, 3(2): 15–23. Published online 15 November 2007. http://www.google.com.au/archives/vol3iss2/0609–030.gram-hanssen.html.

Gram-Hanssen, K. (2008), 'Heat Comfort and Practice Theory: Understanding Everyday Routines of Energy Consumption', in T. G. Ken, A. Tukker, C. Vezzoli and F. Ceschin (eds), *Proceedings 2nd SCORE! Conference: Sustainable Consumption and Production: Framework for Action*, Brussels, Belgium.

Gram-Hanssen, K. (2011), 'Understanding Change and Continuity in Residential Energy Consumption', *Journal of Consumer Culture*, 11(1): 61–78.

Gramazio, F. and M. Kohler (2008), *Digital Materiality in Architecture*, Baden: Lars Müller Publishers.

Gunn, W. and J. Donovan (2012), 'Design Anthropology: An Introduction', in W. Gunn and J. Donovan (eds), *Design and Anthropology*, Farnham: Ashgate.

Gunn, W. and C. Clausen (2013), 'Conceptions of Innovation and Practice(s) of Inhabiting Indoor Climate', in W. Gunn, T. Otto and R. C. Smith (eds), *Design Anthropology: Theory and Practice*, London: Bloomsbury.

Gunn, W., T. Otto and R. C. Smith (eds) (2013), *Design Anthropology: Theory and Practice*, Oxford: Bloomsbury Publishing.

Halse, J. (2013), 'Ethnographies of the Possible', in W. Gunn, T. Otto and R.C. Smith (eds), *Design Anthropology: Theory and Practice*, London: Bloomsbury.

Hanson, S. and G. Pratt (1988), 'Reconceptualizing the links between home and work in urban geography', *Economic Geography*, 64(4): 299–321.

Harris, M. (2007), 'Introduction: Ways of Knowing', in M. Harris (ed.), *Ways of Knowing, New Approaches in the Anthropology of Experience and Learning*, Oxford: Berghahn.

Harrison, S., D. Tatar and P. Sengers (2007), 'The three paradigms of HCI', in *Proceedings of the SIGCHI Conference on Human Factors in Computing Systems*, ACM Press: New York.

Harrison, S., D. Tatar and P. Sengers (2007), The three paradigms of HCI. In *Alt. chi. Proceedings of CHI '07*. ACM Press: New York.

Hauge, B. (2013), 'The air from outside: Getting to know the world through air practices', *Journal of Material Culture*, 18(2): 171–87.

Heyl, S. (2001), 'Ethnographic Interviewing', in P. Atkinson, A. Coffey, S. Delamont, J. Lofland and L. Lofland (eds), *Handbook of Ethnography*, London: Sage.

Hinton, E., K. Bickerstaff and H. Bulkeley (2012), Understanding and changing comfort practices. Report from the Carbon, Control and Comfort (CCC) project, King's College London.

Hjorth, L. and S. Pink (2014), 'New visualities and the digital wayfarer: Reconceptualizing camera phone photography and locative media', *Mobile Media and Communication*, 2: 40–57.

Horst, Heather A. (2006), 'Building Home: Being and Becoming a Returned Resident', in D. Plaza and F. Henry (eds), *Returning to the Source: The Final Stage of the Caribbean Migration Circuit*, Mona: University of the West Indies Press.

Horst, H. (2008), 'Planning to forget: Mobility and violence in urban jamaica', *Social Anthropology/Anthropologie Sociale*, 16(1): 51–62.

Horst, Heather A. (2011), 'Reclaiming Place: The Architecture of Home, Family and Migration', *Anthropologica: Journal of the Canadian Anthropological Society*, 53(1): 29–39.

Horst, H. A. (2012), 'New Media Technologies in Everyday Life', in H. Horst and D. Miller (eds), *Digital Anthropology*, 61–79, London: Berg.

Horst, H. (2014a), 'Calling My Name: Sound, Orality and The cell Phone Contact List', in S. Gopinath and J. Stanyek (eds), *The Oxford Handbook of Mobile Music Studies*, Volume 1, 201–10, Oxford University Press, New York, United States.

Horst, H. (2016), 'Mobile Intimacies: Everyday Design and the Aesthetics of Mobile Phones', In *Digital Materialities: Design and Anthropology*, Bloomsbury Publishing, United Kingdom.

Horst, H. A. and D. Miller (eds) (2012), *Digital Anthropology*, London: Bloomsbury.

Horst, H. and E. Taylor (2014), 'The Role of Mobile Phones in the Mediation of Border Crossings: A Study of Haiti and the Dominican Republic', *The Australian Journal of Anthropology*, 25(2): 155–70.

Hunt, J. (2010), 'Prototyping the Social: Temporality and Speculative Futures at the Intersection of Design and Culture', in A. Clark (ed.), *Design Anthropology*, New York/Wien: Springer Verlag.

Ingold T (2000), *The Perception of the Environment*, London: Routledge.

Ingold, T. (2007), *A Brief History of the Line*, London: Routledge.

Ingold, T. (2008a), 'Bindings Against Boundaries: Entanglements of Life in an Open World', *Environment and Planning A*, 40: 1796–181.

Ingold, T. (2008b), 'Bringing Things to Life: Creative Entanglements in a World of Materials', ESRC National Centre for Research Methods, NCRM Working Paper Series, 1–15.

Ingold, T. (2010), 'Footprints through the Weather-World: Walking, Breathing, Knowing', *Journal of the Royal Anthropological Institute*, 16 (s1): S121–S139.

Ingold, T. (2011), *Being Alive: Essays on Movement, Knowledge and Description*, Oxford: Routledge.

Ingold, T. (2011), 'Reply to David Howes', *Social Anthropology*, 19(3): 323–7.

Ingold, T. (2012), 'Introduction: The Perception of the User–producer', in W. Gunn and J. Donovan (eds), *Design and Anthropology*, Farnham: Ashgate

Ingold, T. and E. Hallam (2007), *Creativity and Cultural Improvisation*, Oxford: Berg.

Ingram, J., E. Shove and M. Watson (2007), 'Products and Practices: Selected Concepts from Science and Technology Studies and from Social Theories of Consumption and Practice', *Design Issues*, 23(2): 3–16.

Irani, L. and P. Dourish (2009), 'Postcolonial Interculturality', IWIC'09, 20–21 February 2009, Palo Alto, California, USA. ACM 978-1-60558-502-4/09/02.

Irving, A. (2017), 'The Art of Turning Left and Right', in J. F. Salazar, S. Pink, A. Irving and J. Sjoberg (eds), *Future Anthropologies*, London: Bloomsbury.

Johnson, L. C., J. Andrey and S. M. Shaw (2007), 'Mr. Dithers Comes to Dinner: Telework and the Merging of Women's Work and Home Domains in Canada', *Gender, Place and Culture*, 14(2): 141–61.

Keightly, E. (2012), 'Introduction: Time, Media, Modernity', in E. Keightly (ed.), *Time, Media and Modernity*, Basingstoke: Palgrave Macmillan.

Keightley, E., M. Pickering and N. Allett (2012), 'The Self-Interview: A New Method in Social Science Research', *International Journal of Social Research Methodology*, 15(6): 507–21.

Kinsley, S. (2011), 'Anticipating Ubiquitous Computing: Logics to Forecast Technological Futures', *Geoforum*, 42(2): 231–40.

Kinsley, S. (2012), 'Futures in the Making: Practices to Anticipate "Ubiquitous Computing" Environment and Planning A', 44: 1554–69.

Kitchin, R. and M. Dodge (2011), *Code/Space. Software and Everyday Life*, Boston, MA: MIT Press.

Kjærsgaard, M. and T. Otto (2012), 'Anthropological Fieldwork and Designing Potentials', in W. Gunn and J. Donovan (eds), *Design and Anthropology*, 177–91, Surrey, UK: Ashgate.

Kuijer, L., A. de Jong and D. van Wijk (2013), 'Practices as a Unit of Design: An Exploration of Theoretical Guidelines in a Study on Bathing', *Transactions on Computer-Human Interaction* 20(4). Article no. 21.

Lanzeni, D. (2016), 'Smart Global Futures: Designing Affordable Materialities For A Better Life', in S. Pink, E. Ardevol and D. Lanzeni (eds), *Digital Materialities: Anthropology and Design*, London: Bloomsbury.

Law, L. (2001), 'Home Cooking: Filipino Women and Geographies of the Senses in Hong Kong', *Cultural Geographies*, 8(3): 264–83.

Law, J. (2004), *After Method: Mess in Social Science Research*, London: Routledge.

Leavy, P. (2015), *Method Meets Art: Arts-Based Research Practice*, New York: Guilford Press.

Leder Mackley, K. and S. Pink (2013), 'From Emplaced Knowing to Interdisciplinary Knowledge: Sensory Ethnography in Energy Research', *Senses and Society*, 8(3): 335–53.

Leder Mackley, K. and S. Pink (2017), 'From Emplaced Knowing to Interdisciplinary Knowledge: Sensory Ethnography in Energy Research', in V. Fors, T. O'Dell and S. Pink (eds), *Working in the Between: Theoretical Scholarship and Applied Practice*, Oxford: Berghahn.

Lilley, D., T. A. Bhamra, V. Haines and V. Mitchell (2010), *6th International Symposium on Environmentally Conscious Design and Inerse Manufacturing*, Sapporo, Japan, 7–9 December 2010.

Lindtner, S., K. Anderson and P. Dourish (2012), 'Cultural Appropriation: Information Technologies as Sites of Transnational Imagination', *CSCW* 2012, 11–15 February 2012, Seattle, Washington, USA. Copyright 2011 ACM 978-1-4503-1086-4/12/02.

Lorimer, H. (2005), 'Cultural Geography: The Busyness of Being "More Than Representational"', *Progress in Human Geography*, 29(1): 83–94.

Lupton, D. (2016), *The Quantified Self*, Cambridge: Polity.

Lury, C. and N. Wakeford (2012), *Inventive Methods: The Happening of the Social*, Oxford: Routledge.

MacDougall, D. (1997), 'The Visual in Anthropology', in M. Banks and H. Morphy (eds), *Rethinking Visual Anthropology*, 276–95, New Haven and London: Yale University Press.

MacDougall, D. (1998), *Transcultural Cinema*, Princeton: Princeton University Press.

Madianou, M. and D. Miller (2012), *Migration and New Media: Transnational Families and Polymedia*, London: Routledge.

Mallaband, B., V. Haines and V. Mitchell (2013), 'Exploring Past Home Improvement Experiences To Develop Future Energy Saving Technologies', in *ACM SIGCHI Conference on Human Factors in Computing Systems (CHI), Methods for Studying Technology in the Home Workshop*, Paris, France, 27 April to 27–23 May 2013, p. 4.

Maller, C and Y. Strengers (2013), 'The Global Migration of Everyday Life: Investigating the Practice Memories of Australian Migrants', *Geoforum*, 44: 243–52.

Malnar J and F. Vodvarka (2004), *Sensory Design*, Minneapolis, MI: University of Minnesota Press.

Martens, L. (2012), 'The Politics and Practices of Looking: CCTV Video and Domestic Kitchen Practices', in S. Pink (ed.), *Advances in Visual Methodology*, London: Sage.

Martens, L., B. Halkier and S. Pink (2014), 'Researching Habits: Advances In Linguistic And Embodied Research Practice', *International Journal of Social Research Methodology*, doi:10.1080/13645579.2014.853999.

Martens, L. and S. Scott (2004), Domestic Kitchen Practices: Routines, Risks and Reflexivity, ESRC End of Award Report, 1–52.

Massey, D. (2005), *For Space*, London: Sage.

Mellick Lopes, A. and A. Gill (2015), 'Reorienting Sustainable Design: Practice Theory and Aspirational Conceptions of Use', *Journal of Design Research*, 13(3): 248–64.

Merriman, P. (2012), *Mobility, Space, and Culture*, London: Routledge.

Michael, M. (2016), 'Speculative Design and Digital Materialities: Idiocy, Threat and Com-Promise', in S. Pink, E. Ardevol and D. Lanzeni (eds), *Digital Materialities: Anthropology and Design*, London: Bloomsbury.

Miller, D. (1988), 'Appropriating the State in the Council Estate', *Man*, 23: 353–72.

Miller, D. (ed.) (2001), *Home Possessions*, Oxford: Berg.

Mills, D. (2005), 'Dinner at Claridges? Anthropology and the "Captains of Industry", 1947–55', in S. Pink (ed.), *Applications of Anthropology: Professional Anthropology in the Twenty-first Century*, New York: Berghahn Books.

Mitchell, V., K. Leder Mackley, S. Pink, G. Wilson, et al. (2015), 'Situating Digital Interventions: Mixed Methods for HCI Research in the Home', *Interacting with Computers*, 27 (1): 3–12. doi:10.1093/iwc/iwu034.

Moores, S. (2012), 'Media, Place and Mobility', Basingstoke, UK: Palgrave Macmillan.

Morley, D. (2000), *Home Territories. Media, Mobility and Identity*, London and New York: Routledge.

Morley, D. (2009), 'For a Materialist, Non-Media-Centric Media Studies', *Television & New Media*, 10(1): 114–16.

Moroşanu, R. (2016a), *An Ethnography of Household Energy Demand in the UK: Everyday Temporalities of Digital Media Usage*, Basingstoke: Palgrave Macmillan.

Moroşanu, R. (2016b), 'Making Multitemporality with Character Houses: Time Trickery, Ethical Practice, and Energy Demand in Postcolonial Britain', *The Cambridge Journal of Anthropology*, 34(1): 113–24.

Muir, S. and J. Mason (2012), 'Capturing Christmas: The Sensory Potential of Data from Participant Produced Video', *Sociological Research Online*, 17(1): 5. Available online at http://www.socresonline.org.uk/17/1/5.html, accessed 13 July 2017.

Nippert-Eng, C. E. (2008), *Home and Work: Negotiating Boundaries through Everyday Life*, Chicago: University of Chicago Press.

O'Dell, T. and R. Willim (2011), 'Irregular Ethnographies: An Introduction', *Ethnologia Europaea*, 41(1): 5–14.

O'Reilly, K. (2005), *Ethnographic Research*, London: Routledge.

Oakley, A. (2000), *Experiments in Knowing: Gender and Method in The Social Sciences*, Cambridge: Polity.

Otto, T. and C. Smith (2013), 'Design Anthropology: A Distinct Style of Knowing', in W. Gunn, T. Otto and R. C. Smith (eds), *Design Anthropology: Theory and Practice*, Oxford: Bloomsbury Publishing.

Paay, J., J. Kjeldskov and M. B. Skov (2015), 'Connecting in the Kitchen: An Empirical Study of Physical Interactions while Cooking Together at Home', *Proceedings of the 18th ACM Conference on Computer Supported Cooperative Work & Social Computing, CSCW '15, Vancouver, 14–18 March 2015*, ACM, New York, 276–87.

Pallasmaa, J. (1994), 'Identity, Intimacy and Domocile: Notes on the Phenomenology of Home in Rkkitenti', *Finnish Architectural Review*, 1. http://www.uiah.fi/studies/history2/eident.htm, accessed 15 August 2015.

Pallasmaa, J. (2009), *The Thinking Hand: Existential and Embodied Wisdom in Architecture*, Chichester, UK: Wiley.

Palmer, J. and I. Cooper (2013), United Kingdom housing energy fact file. Department of Energy and Climate Change. https://www.gov.uk/government/uploads/system/uploads/attachment_data/file/345141/uk_housing_fact_file_2013.pdf, accessed 21 June 2016.

Pels, P. (2000), 'The Trickster's Dilemma: Ethics and the Technologies of the Anthropological Self', in M. Strathern (ed.), *Audit Cultures: Anthropological Studies in Accountability*, London: Routledge

Petridou, E. (2001), 'The Taste of Home', in D. Miller (ed.), *Home Possessions*, Oxford: Berg

Pink, S. (2004), *Home Truths: Gender, Domestic Objects and Everyday Life*, Oxford: Berg.

Pink, S. (2012), 'Domestic Time in the Sensory Home: On Knowing in Practice in The Bathroom', in E. Keightly (ed.), *Time, Media and Modernity*, 184–200, Basingstoke: Palgrave.

Pink, S. (2012), *Situating Everyday Life: Practices and Places*, London: Sage.

Pink, S. (2013), *Doing Visual Ethnography*, Revised and expanded 3rd edition, London: Sage

Pink, S. (2015), *Doing Sensory Ethnography*, second edition, London: Sage.

Pink, S. (2017), 'Ethics in a Changing World: Embracing Uncertainty, Understanding Futures, and Making Responsible Interventions', in S. Pink,

V. Fors, T. O'Dell (eds), *Working in the Between: Theoretical Scholarship And Applied Practice*, Oxford: Berghahn.

Pink, S. and V. Fors (2017), 'Being in a Mediated World: Self-tracking and the Mind-body-environment', *Cultural Geographies*. Online first doi:10.1177/1474474016684127.

Pink, S. and K. Leder Mackley (2012), 'Video as a Route to Sensing Invisible Energy', *Sociological Research Online*, February 2012, on line at http://www.socresonline.org.uk/17/1/3.html

Pink, S. and K. Leder Mackley (2013), 'Saturated and Situated: Rethinking Media in Everyday Life', *Media, Culture and Society*, 35(6): 677–91. doi 10.1177/0163443713491298.

Pink, S. and K. Leder Mackley (2014a), 'Flow in Everyday Life: Situating Practices', in C. Maller and Y. Strengers (eds), *Beyond Behaviour Change: Intervening in Social Practices for Sustainability*, London: Routledge.

Pink, S. and K. Leder Mackley (2014b), 'Reenactment Methodologies for Everyday Life Research: Art Therapy Insights for Video Ethnography', *Visual Studies*, 29(2): 146–54.

Pink, S. and K. Leder Mackley (2015), 'Social Science, Design And Everyday Life: Refiguring Showering Through Anthropological Ethnography', *Journal of Design Research*, 13(3): 278–92.

Pink, S. and K. Leder Mackley (2016), 'Moving, Making and Atmosphere: Routines of Home as Sites for Mundane Improvisation', *Mobilities*, 11(02): 171–87.

Pink, S. and J. Morgan (2013), 'Short Term Ethnography: Intense Routes to Knowing', *Symbolic Interaction*, 36(3): 351–61.

Pink, S. and J. Postill (2016), 'Student Migration and Domestic Improvisation: Understanding Transient Migration though the Experience of Everyday Laundry', *Transitions*, 1(1): 13–28.

Pink, S. and J. F. Salazar (2017), 'Anthropology and Futures: Setting the Agenda', in J. F. Salazar, S. Pink, A. Irving and J. Sjoberg (eds), *Future Anthropologies*, London: Bloomsbury.

Pink, S., K. Leder Mackley, V. Mitchell, C. Escobar-Tello, M. Hanratty, T. Bhamra and R. Moroşanu (2013), 'Applying the Lens of Sensory Ethnography to Sustainable HCI', *Transactions on Computer-Human Interaction*, 20(4). Article no. 25. http://dl.acm.org/citation.cfm?doid=2494261

Pink, S., K. Leder Mackley and R. Moroşanu (2015), 'Hanging Out at Home: Laundry as a Thread and Texture of Everyday Life', *International Journal of Cultural Studies*, 18(2): 209–24.

Pink, S., K. Leder Mackley and R. Moroşanu (2015), 'Researching Atmospheres: Video, Knowing, Feeling and Temporality', *Visual Communication*, 14(3): 351–69. doi:10.1177/1470357215579580.

Pink, S., J. Morgan and A. Dainty (2015), 'Other People's Homes as Sites of Uncertainty: Ways of Knowing and Being Safe', *Environment and Planning A*, 47(2): 450–64.

Pink, S. and Y. Akama and contributors (2015), *Un/Certainty*. iBook, download from http://d-e-futures.com/projects/uncertainty/

Pink, S., E. Ardevol and D. Lanzeni (2016), 'Digital Materiality: Configuring A Field of Anthropology/Design?' in S. Pink, E. Ardevol and D. Lanzeni (eds), *Digital Materialities: Anthropology and Design*, Oxford: Bloomsbury

Pink, S., J. Sinanan, L. Hjorth and H. Horst (2016), 'Tactile Digital Ethnography: Researching Mobile Media through the Hand', *Mobile Media and Communication* 4(2): 237–51.

Pink, S., K. Leder Mackley, V. Mitchell, G. Wilson and T. Bhamra (2016), 'Refiguring Digital Interventions for Energy Demand Reduction: Designing for Life in the Digital Material Home', in S. Pink, E. Ardevol and D. Lanzeni (eds), *Digital Materialities: Anthropology and Design*, Oxford: Bloomsbury.

Pink, S. H. Horst, J. Postill, L. Hjorth, T. Lewis and J. Tacchi (2016), *Digital Ethnography: Principles and Practice*, London: Sage.

Pink, S., L. Hjorth, H. Horst, J. Nettheim and G. Bell (2017), 'Digital Play in the Home: Play, Playbour and Labour', *European Journal of Cultural Studies*.

Porteous, C. D. A., T. R. Sharpe, R. Menon, D. Shearer, H. Musa, P. H. Baker, C. Sanders, P. A. Strachan, N. J. Kelly and A. Markopoulos (2014), 'Domestic Laundering: Environmental Audit in Glasgow with Emphasis on Passive Indoor Drying and Air Quality', *Indoor and Built Environment*, 23: 373.

Pratt, G. (1999), 'From Registered Nurse to Registered Nanny: Discursive Geographies of Filipina Domestic Workers in Vancouver, B.C.', *Economic Geography*, 75(3): 215–36.

Rapley, T. (2004), 'Interviews', in C. Seale, G. Gobo, J. F. Gubrium and D. Silverman (eds), *Qualitative Research Practice*, London: Sage.

Rapport, N. and A. Dawson (eds) (1998), *Migrants of Identity: Perceptions of 'Home' in a World of Movement*, Oxford: Berg.

Reckwitz, A. (2002), 'Towards a Theory of Social Practices: A Development in Culturalist Theorizing', *European Journal of Social Theory*, 5(2): 243–63.

Salazar, J.F., S. Pink, A. Irving and J. Sjoberg (eds) (2017), *Future Anthropologies*, London: Bloomsbury.

Schatzki, T. (2001), 'Introduction: Practice Theory', in T. Schatzki, K. Knorr-Cetina and E. von Savigny (eds), *The Practice Turn in Social Theory*, London: Routledge.

Sengers, P., K. Boehner and N. Knouf (2009), Sustainable HCI meets third wave HCI: 4 themes. CHI 2009 workshop.

Shaw, R. (2014), 'Controlling Darkness: Self, Dark and the Domestic Night', *Cultural Geographies*. Published online 20 June 2014. doi:10.1177/1474474014539250.

Shove, E. (2003), *Comfort, Convenience and Cleanliness*, Oxford: Berg.

Shove, E., M. Watson, M. Hand and J. Ingram (2007), *The Design of Everyday Life*, Oxford: Berg.

Silverstone, R. and E. Hirsch (eds), *Consuming Technologies: Media and Information in Domestic Spaces*, London: Routledge.

Skinner, J. (ed.) (2012), *The Interview: An Ethnographic Approach*, Oxford: Bloomsbury.

Smith, P. R. (2011), 'The Pitfalls of Home: Protecting the Health and Safety of Paid Domestic Workers', *Canadian Journal of Women and the Law/Revue Femmes et Droit*, 23(1): 309–39.

Smith, R. C. and M. G. Kjærsgaard (2015), 'Design Anthropology in Participatory Design', *Interaction Design and Architecture(s) Journal – IxD&A*, N.26, 2015, pp. 73–80. Online at: http://pure.au.dk/portal/files/96923075/Design_Anthropology_IxDA_26_P_FS.pdf, accessed 15 May 2016.

Sneath, D., M. Holbraad and M. A.Pedersen (2009), 'Technologies of the Imagination: An Introduction', *Ethnos: Journal of Anthropology*, 74(1): 5–30.

Sperschneider, W. (2007), 'Video Ethnography under Industrial Constraints: Observational Techniques and Video Analysis', in S. Pink (ed.) *Visual Interventions*, Oxford: Berghahn.

Strathern, M. (2000), 'Afterword: Accountability ... And Ethnography', in M. Strathern (ed.), *Audit Cultures: Anthropological Studies in Accountability*, London: Routledge

Strengers, Y. (2013), *Smart Energy Technologies in Everyday Life: Smart Utopia?*, Palgrave Macmillan, New York.

Strengers, Y. (2016), 'Envisioning the Smart Home: Reimagining a Smart Energy Future', in S. Pink, E. Ardevol and D. Lanzeni (eds), *Digital Materailies: Anthropology and Design*, Bloomsbury: London.

Sunderland, P. and R. Denny (2009), *Doing Anthropology in Consumer Research*, Walnut Creek: Left Coast Press.

Swan, L., A. S. Taylor and R. Harper (2008), Making place for clutter and other ideas of home. ACM Transactions on Computer-Human Interaction (TOCHI), 15(2), 9.

Taylor, B. J. and M. Donnelly (2006), 'Risks to Home Care Workers: Professional Perspectives', *Health, Risk and Society*, 8(3), 239–56.

Taylor, A.S., R. Harper, L. Swan, S. Izadi, A. Sellen and M. Perry (2007), 'Homes That Make us Smart', *Personal Ubiquitous Computing*, 11: 383–93.

Thrift, N.J. (2008), *Non-Representational Theory: Space, Politics, Affect*, London: Routledge.

Tolia-Kelly, D. P. (2010), *Landscape, Race and Memory: Material Ecologies of Citizenship*, Farnham: Ashgate.

Tolmie, P., J. Pycock, T. Diggins, A. MacLean and A. Karsenty (2002), 'Unremarkable Computing', in *Proceedings of the SIGCHI Conference on Human Factors in Computing Systems (CHI '02)*. ACM, New York, NY, 399–406.

van Dijck, J. (2004), 'Composing the Self: Of Diaries and Lifelogs', *The Fibreculture Journal*, 3. http://three.fibreculturejournal.org/fcj-012-composingthe-self-of-diaries-and-lifelogs/, accessed 14 April 2015.

Willmann, J., F. Gramazio, M. Kohler and S. Langenberg (2013), 'Digital by Material', in S. Brell-Cokcan and J. Braumann (eds), *Robotic Fabrication in Architecture, Art and Design,* 12–27, Vienna: Springer.

Wright, S. (2005), 'Machetes into a Jungle? A History of Anthropology in Policy and Practice, 1981–2000', in S. Pink (ed.), *Applications of Anthropology: Professional Anthropology in the Twenty-first Century*, 27–54, New York: Berghahn Books.

Index